OMG

I NEED A JOB

A Practical Guide to
Finding a Great Job in Any Economy

D1733380

Bob Braham

OMG I NEED A JOB

 Robertson Publishing™
www.RobertsonPublishing.com

To purchase additional copies of this book go to:
amazon.com
barnesandnoble.com

Acknowledgements

To my wife, Carol, my daughter, Kate, and my son, John, without whose inspiration and support I would not have written this book or enjoyed my career journey.

There have been many people with whom I've networked to achieve my own career success. Thank you for giving me your support, time, and insights.

TABLE OF CONTENTS

FOREWORD

By John Gorman,
former Chief Operating Officer, Taco Bell

Reading OMG I Need a Job, reminded me of Taco Bell. We started our first stand in Southern California in 1951. It wasn't easy. We had to roll up our sleeves and leverage our relationships across the industry to make it work. We didn't even start with tacos. We started with hamburgers and realized that we could further differentiate ourselves from our competition by switching to tacos. The business grew slowly at first, just one taco stand at a time until we accelerated to our sale to PepsiCo Inc., with almost 900 restaurants in 1978. Today, over 6,000 Taco Bells in the United States alone serve 37 million people each week, and we are expanding internationally.

Bob's career has followed the same path of determination. As a fresh-scrubbed kid out of Duke University making his mark in the sales organization of Hewlett-Packard, Bob rose through the ranks at HP. After he left, he continued to progress in his career, and we talked frequently about leadership and business. Bob was always a willing listener. We frequently had long discussions over breakfast or lunch in downtown Yorba Linda, California.

When Bob had an opportunity to leave Southern California and move to Silicon Valley, I suggested he jump on it and not look back. Bob was a high-tech manager, and the valley has been the place to be to grow careers in tech. During a recent stretch, he found the going got a little tough. Proving that bad things really do happen to good people, Bob found himself being let go several times and conducting the well-known job search. Even though he had moved away, Bob and I continued to talk about the moves he was making as he was experiencing career churn. Ironically, each job move placed him in a better position than he'd been in before. He quickly grew from a manager to a director to a vice president, and as he grew in his career, others sought him out for his advice on their own job searches.

Many people would have quit and settled for something easy while making adjustments in their lifestyles. However, Bob had obligations in the community. As an active member of his church and town and as a board member of Catholic Charities of Santa Clara County, he had opportunities to help others, and he wanted to continue to participate in those activities.

Many books have been written on the topic of the job search. I don't think that any of these books have been authored by somebody who has embraced the process like Bob. Those reading this book will learn something new in their approach to landing a great position. I applaud him for seeing this book through and for helping others achieve opportunities in their careers.

Preface

Welcome to the world of job seekers — one that can be difficult to navigate. Schools have thoroughly trained us in disciplines such as science, language, and arithmetic. They've taught some of us vocations, or at least sets of skills that enable us to do jobs. Rarely, however, have they instructed us how to find jobs.

Much has been written about the job-seeking world. Between 2008 and 2013, unemployment stalled between 8 and 10 percent. Additionally, nearly 20 percent of people working are underemployed.[1] Some 75 percent of all people employed are classified as job seekers actively searching for new job opportunities.[2]

Job seeking frequently creates stress. There are difficulties to endure, such as the pain of rejection, anxiety over getting interview feedback, and doubts about whether you'll ever find the right job for you.

This process has an upside, though. Job seeking can be a transformational time in your life. The goal of this book is to make that transformation a positive experience by showing you a proven process for navigating the job-search waters. I've been hired and let go a number of times in my career. But each time I lost a job, I found a way to get a new and better one.

---

1. Reuters's Feb. 23, 2010
2. Huffington Post, October 9, 2012

Over time, I documented my findings and developed them into a process that I shared informally with others. Eventually, I realized that many people could use this process to assist them during one of the most stressful times in their careers. In this book, I share my experiences to help you improve your chances of success in your search.

While these insights will hold true in both good times and bad, they'll be critical when you find that the competition for the position you want is brutal. Take heart. This book will help you keep ahead of your job-seeking competition and find your dream job.

Getting Out in Front

The key to navigating the job-search process is to get in front of a hiring manager at the right time in the process. This manager is the person you would directly report to if you worked for the targeted company. So, you need to understand how that hiring manager would operate during a search. While we've described the world of the job seeker, let's look at the job-seeking process from the hiring manager's perspective. Figure 1 illustrates how that manager considers pursuing candidates to fill a job need.

A set of concentric circles depicts the hiring manager's world. Each of these is a little further away from the center—that is, from the actual hiring manager and that individual's own network. The best choice is a candidate from this network, frequently one who has worked for the manager and is, therefore, a low-risk hire; after all, this candidate has a track record and presumably a good relationship with the manager.

Figure 1.

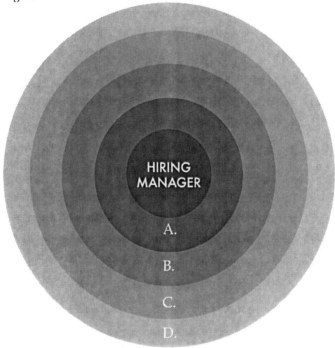

A. *Candidates within Hiring Managers Network.*

B. *Candidates recommended within Hiring Managers' Network.*

C. *Recruiters from Hiring Mangers Network*

D. *Resumes from HR from a job posting.*

Hiring managers generally consider all possible candidates in a circle before moving on to the next one, where there is less of a track record, less of a relationship, and therefore, more of a risk. By the time hiring managers get to the fourth circle, they're exhausted, and the talent pool becomes broad. Your competition is great, and the variables are largely out of your control.

Ideally, you want to be in the first circle, which is where many people focus their networking. The problem is this circle represents a small number of opportunities. So, you should target the second circle, expanding your network to bring you into the process early and with a little tailwind behind you. This book gives you a simple process for getting yourself in front of hiring managers by leveraging a network.

Networking will help you understand an industry's dynamics and hiring practices and focus on the opportunities with the highest probability of success. You'll talk to decision makers before they formally post the job, so you can sell yourself with little or no competition.

Many people tell me they're not outgoing enough to network. They prefer to stay in their homes and research posted openings online then send out as many resumes as they can in what is commonly called the "spray and pray" method.

Replying to these openings is easy but passive. Many newspapers and magazines have cited the low success rate of responding to them, while stating that it's extremely difficult to find a job in a tough economy. It's true that pursuing posted job openings is not the best way to go. But it's not true that finding a job in a challenging economy is difficult. At least it needn't be.

This book takes you through a process that's effective in both good times and bad.

- **Step 1** covers handling the emotional letdown of a job loss and crafting your story.

- **Step 2** provides guidelines for getting yourself organized.

- **Step 3** gives insights into leveraging the web.

- **Step 4** offers a framework to help you with self-assessment and to consider what kind of job you really want.

Networking will serve as the core of your search, provide you with the greatest opportunity to differentiate you from the competition, and get you in the door of the desired company.

- **Step 5** provides a meaty discussion of networking.

- **Steps 6 and 7** cover resume writing and interviewing skills. These are part of the job-search foundation, and while much has been written about them, I provide unique insights to help you stand out from the pack.

- **Step 8** reviews how to handle the hire-offer process and close the deal on your dream job.

Having been through the process many times myself, I share personal accounts as well as several case studies of people I've worked with. The path you're traveling has been taken many times before. There's a recipe for success as well as for failure. Read this book, and you'll be on your way to a successful search.

KICKING OFF MY CAREER

I started my career at Hewlett-Packard in the summer of 1981. I was a freshly minted electrical engineering graduate, having been a member of the national honor society at Duke University. Even back then, Duke was known as a basketball school, with Coach Mike Krzyzewski just starting his well-chronicled career. I had no idea what awaited me in the working world, but I moved from Durham, North Carolina, to Orange County, California, determined to make my mark.

Back in 1981, Hewlett-Packard was what many today refer to as the "Old HP." Bill Hewlett and Dave Packard were alive and very much in control of the company. People worked hard to get in, establish themselves, and grow their careers for life. After all, there was no reason to leave HP. In 1982, the company tied IBM on Fortune magazine's list of the most admired companies in America. HP was a stalwart, yet still-rising, high-tech star. Employees made relationships that lasted a lifetime. Some thirty years after starting at the company, I still keep in touch on a regular basis with people I knew there.

I joined HP as a sales trainee at a branch office in Fullerton, California. I was only twenty-one years old, and, to make matters worse, I looked young for my age. "Bobby Braham," they used to call me. Later I grew a mustache to give myself a little corporate credibility, but while at HP, I was always "Bobby" to somebody.

I remained in the company's sales-training program for one and a half years and was thrust into my first sales territory at the ripe old age of twenty-three. My sales manager was a good guy, who did well over the years at HP. He'd tell me I was like an "uncut diamond in the hands of Michelangelo," and he intended to help me become successful. He guided me to an exceptional start, as I was named HP's Rookie of the Year in Southern California.

He received a promotion to another area, and I got a new boss who'd been a mentor to me during my initial sales tenure. We made loads of sales calls together, followed by lunch at the beach and an occasional Friday night out. The relationship proved fruitful, as I later became the number-one selling rep out of about one hundred in Southern California. The following year, HP named me the Most Valuable Player on the Southern California sales force and entered me into the HP Hall of Fame. Many people, including my first manager, told me I was headed for greatness and might someday be CEO of the company. While I was a classic well-mannered young man, I started to get a little cocky at this stage of my career. I was ambitious and had my sights set high.

Later I became a sales manager under a general manager I'd worked for briefly as a trainee. We got along well, so this had all the makings of a mentor/mentee relationship as I made my way to the top. All part of the master plan of a rising young executive? No, it was the start of seeing the ugly underbelly of the real world. Power and strategic offsite meetings were accompanied by politics and what I later learned was hard, cold life in the sewer.

The general manager was running a new business unit. At most companies, such units require abnormally large investments to grow. After getting off the ground, they're expected to flourish and provide the company with an excellent return on its investment. But the unthinkable happened. The year was 1989—HP's fiftieth anniversary. All over the world, we toasted the company's past and expected future success. But the computer industry experienced a slowdown that year, and HP was not immune to it. Growth slowed, and the company had to lay people off for the first time in its history. Imagine the shock of drinking champagne with your boss and cubicle mates, celebrating the fifty-year anniversary of a company that had been the bedrock of employment, and then seeing many of them terminated only a few months later. Life in the sewer was beginning for me.

One day I was in my boss's office when he informed me that the company had to divest itself of my team. My job now was to find new positions for my team members and myself. Being a good soldier, I sought jobs for my salespeople first then tried to find something for me. I had been given no timetable. Everyone was expected to search for new assignments in areas that needed help, and all of us pulled together to make that happen. I learned, though, that the process took a little longer the higher up a person was in an organization. Moreover, because Bobby Braham was

"Mr. Ambition," no sales manager would approach me with a rep job for fear I'd fly the coop as soon as something better came along. So, while it was easy to find new sales positions for my reps, that wasn't the case for me.

Fortunately, a senior sales executive recruited me to his team, and the move was actually a promotion to a key position on his staff. My longevity and connections had come in handy, and my new role worked out well for two years.

Then more things began to unravel, as additional changes occurred. Ray took another job within the company, and I got a new boss, who came from outside the congenial confines of Southern California, where almost everybody was well acquainted with each other. Although the new boss and I knew each other by name, we had no relationship. That was the first time I had worked for someone with whom I had no history. While the guy seemed like a decent sort, my gut told me I was in trouble. Sure enough, all the signs started pointing in that direction. He excluded me from key meetings. Plum assignments went to men the new leader had worked with in the past, leaving the leftovers to me. Finally, he passed me over for a raise. Clearly, the time had come for me to conclude my stay with Hewlett-Packard.

But first I talked it over with my wife. Somehow, I knew that, although departing was the right thing to do, it would change my career forever. I'd be leaving a company at which I had the system wired and where I'd developed relationships. It would be difficult, but

I decided to leave anyway.

I moved from Southern California to Silicon Valley for stints with Sun Microsystems—where an executive I knew from HP had hired me—and a couple of start-ups. But the period of employment that moved me to write this book was 2008–2010, when I held executive positions with two different companies. At both, the hiring manager left within three months of my joining, and I was let go. For a man who was no longer carefree Bobby Braham but rather a husband with a mortgage, kids entering college, and a stressed wife trying to run a household, this was awful. Yet it led to my greatest breakthrough.

Each time a company released me, my job search became my full-time passion. I learned how to look for a new position and became extremely good at it. And this was during a tumultuous time, when the country suffered a financial meltdown (now known as the Great Recession), and unemployment soared. But even in a down economy, I had landed better jobs than I'd had previously.

As I write this book, my most recent position was vice president of marketing at a $20 billion high-tech company with over 50,000 employees and a presence throughout the world. Getting there was a journey—one that I've shared many times over lunch and coffee, at parties, on the phone, and with visitors in my home. Eventually I began to wonder whether the techniques I'd developed were unique. The answer came one day when I received a call from an executive who'd been the CMO at a well-known

Silicon Valley high-tech company. A mutual business associate, who had followed my career and appreciated how I'd moved upward with each new job, referred me to him. The executive had just left a firm that another company had acquired. Over coffee he revealed that he'd been with the company for over twenty years, and while he knew marketing, he had little idea how to look for a new job. He was extraordinarily humble as he asked me how to initiate the process. We discussed my experiences and lessons that I'd learned over the years. So, here was a senior executive, whom I'd looked up to for years, now listening to my advice. I realized then that I had a story to tell and insights to share.

I'll walk you through the essentials of searching for your next job as well as give you an understanding of the hiring process. With a handbook like this, the journey isn't difficult. But keep in mind that, to be successful, you'll also need perseverance and a little courage.

STEP 1: OH NO, I'VE BEEN LET GO— GET READY TO DEVELOP YOUR STORY

So you've been let go from your job. Why? What happened? What's your story? You must develop an explanation for your termination that you're comfortable with and can deliver immediately upon beginning your search. You'll need it for interviews, networking meetings, and social gatherings. You'll have to articulate what happened with confidence, so you can move on and project the appropriate image for your next exciting opportunity. Start with anything you can deliver. As you meet more people who have walked in your shoes, you'll be amazed at how much more comfortable you are in relating the story. When describing my job movement, I got to where I was at ease telling people I had a new boss from the outside who "freed up my career options." Even during interviews, hiring managers appreciated my candor and sense of humor.

Suddenly finding yourself without work can be a tough experience. Here are several typical reasons it can happen:

- A new boss arrives, maybe from the outside. Perhaps he or she has a different way of doing things or brought along a loyal lieutenant to replace you.

- You're one of many people the company has laid

off. The cause may have been an acquisition or a business downturn. Sometimes entire departments are disbanded at one time.

- You have a performance issue. This can sting, because someone has determined that you've failed. You may even feel "less than" as a result. Such a reaction is common. But hang tough, and say merely that the job was not a match.

- You want to advance in your career. You may not have been laid off, but you believe it's time to leverage your talent and ability and look for your next professional opportunity. Or perhaps you've changed, or the job has changed, or the market has. For whatever reason, you want to move on. If you put your mind to it, you can do so by optimizing the experience gained at your previous employer.

How do you proceed? To begin with, keep one maxim in mind: Always be candid; always be confident. In the following chapters, you'll gain the knowledge necessary to move the ball forward in your job search. This will build the confidence you need to land your next job, which could pay more, carry a more substantial title, and offer more responsibility than the one you left, no matter how the economy is doing.

Sometimes you'll encounter people who don't understand how anyone could have been without a job more than once in a recent period. They'll say you've done "too much jumping around." Look at the background of your potential hiring manager. If you go into the interview having had three positions over the past six years (with no contacts recommending you), and the hiring manager has been with two companies in a twenty-five-year career, you'll need to be an absolute star in the interview to overcome his or her conservative tendencies.

I once had an interview with an executive who'd been with the same company for fifteen years. I, on the other hand…well, let's just say I'd moved around a little. Not only could he not get past that, I realized at meeting's end that I wouldn't enjoy working for him. He'd grown up in the organization, essentially as a little boy, and had advanced on the coattails of another successful executive. He was like a nice house pet. I was — and am — more of a maverick. Game over.

In today's job market, people move around all the time. Business acceleration due to the Internet, global competition, and impatient directors demanding faster results has made job-hopping more common and less frowned upon by hiring managers. Rarely do you hear the employment-for-life stories once so common at HP, IBM, General Motors, and Boeing. And because the business world sees so much more job movement today, you don't have to apologize for your situation. You simply need to have a plan to get in front of hiring managers and explain how you can help them improve their organizations based on your own track record.

But just as people move around more today, companies are more prone to fill key positions with outside people. I once found a terrific job only to see my boss resign one month later. The new guy made clear from the start he would run things his own way with his own people. Although I got along well with the executive team, he sent me packing a few weeks after he hired my eventual replacement. I went on to find another job, even better than the one I'd left. This time my hiring manager lasted all of one quarter. The new executive was a high-profile hire, and I received e-mails from many colleagues that, in effect, said, "Oh no, not again!" Sure enough, though I lasted a little longer than last time, this manager, too, freed up my career options.

Fired, downsized, laid off, career options freed up— call it what you will, losing a job is a difficult experience that may shatter your confidence. No need to dissect the experience here. We know what it's about and what it feels like. The question is, how do you get yourself through the emotional ups and downs of this process?

First of all, ask yourself what you did to contribute to the situation. Once when I was let go, the boss walked me through the rationale. Oh, it was nothing personal, he said, explaining that I'd been doing good work, but he had failed to protect me. Still, I said, "When I leave here, I'd like to walk away with something I learned that I can take with me to my next job. Tell me what I did to contribute to the situation." Wow, did I get an earful of insights that I later used to explain what happened and what I'd learned at this company.

When you're interviewing at a company, if you had

performance issues at your previous employer, you can simply say the job was not a match for your skills, but what you learned was:

1. To probe more deeply during the interview process, so you don't just land a job but one that you know you can be successful at.

2. Experience within your field is critical.
   Example: Although I had an excellent track record selling lawn mowers, I thought I'd try something different and sell cruise-ship vacations. While it seemed like a good idea at the time for both me and the company, the economy turned south, and I didn't have the ramp-up time I thought I would have. Thus, I learned that for me, it's better to stay within my area of expertise so I can hit the ground running for my new boss.

Next, give yourself forty-eight hours to grieve, and then get out and get talking. You'll be amazed at the number of people you meet who have been through something similar.

I remember how devastated I felt once when notified that I'd been let go and had an hour and a half to clean out my desk, after which I'd be escorted from the building by a human resources rep. I not only felt embarrassed, I thought my career was essentially over. But then I became part of an outplacement group, and I'll never forget the first meeting I attended just two days later. The group had been meeting weekly and clearly had formed a strong community. That morning there were about twenty people in the room, all seeking outplacement counseling.

They had arrived early and were exchanging stories, not only about their job searches but about their families, vacations, sports, and the like. While the group's enthusiasm was impressive, all I could think about was that I'd now become lumped in with a group of people who were unwanted in the employment world. It felt awful. What had become of me?

The group's leader asked new participants to introduce themselves. There were five of us, and the first two did as requested without much fanfare. Then a remarkable young woman stood up and said she was Nancy and had an MBA from a well-known university in Northern California and eight to ten years' experience in marketing. Then she informed us this was the second time in a year she'd been through the outplacement service. As she revealed her background, I was stunned by how often Nancy had been let go and the short duration of each job. Further, she'd worked at a number of companies that I considered solid — places where longer stays might be expected. As she continued to speak, Nancy struck me as one of the most poised and articulate people I'd ever seen. She was extremely positive and self-confident; there was no doubt in her mind that she would land a job again. I found myself gaining energy from her presentation. Here was a winner who'd gone through more turmoil than I had — and she was ready for more.

I decided I had to get to know Nancy, maybe enlist her on my team once I found a position. Now I was back in the game. I had to leave the meeting early, so at the risk of coming off as a pickup artist, I wrote a hasty note and gave it to her before departing. I had provided a snapshot of my background and invited her to discuss employment opportunities with me over coffee. Nancy called that afternoon, and we got together to exchange ideas.

We stayed in touch for two years, helping each other during the job-search process and comparing notes on the industry. Our get-togethers energized us. Finally, I had an opportunity to hire Nancy, but I was a tad too late. She'd signed with a competitor — a company I had helped her network with.

Let's conclude this section by identifying some common ups and downs faced by job seekers. Knowing that others have gone through these peaks and valleys should provide a little comfort.

Figure 2.

Your Ups
↑   Getting an Interview.
↑   Being Called for a Follow Up Interview.
↑   Having a Great Networking Meeting.
↑   Receiving an Offer.

Your Downs
↓   Being Rejected in an Interview.
↓   Having a Great Interview but NOT hearing back from the Company.
↓   Having a Networking Meeting that is So Bad that it Saps Your Energy.
↓   Working for Several Days with No Active Interviews or Opportunities. This may pitch you into outright despair.

A key to successful job searching is to manage your emotions. The rule is don't let your highs get too high or your lows too low. If you can manage your emotions and stay focused, believe it or not, you'll find the process exhilarating. And that exhilaration will help you land a super job and realize that your previous employer actually did you a favor by laying you off.

STEP 2: GET ORGANIZED

Stay on Track

The search for employment is now your full-time job. That's right. You need to dedicate eight or nine hours a day to this process. Your workday will include:

1. Researching companies on the web (covered in Step 3).

2. Researching contacts on LinkedIn (also in Step 3).

3. Making networking calls (Step 5).

4. Conducting networking interviews (Step 5).

5. Attending networking events (Step 5).

6. Going on job interviews (Step 7).

7. Writing thank-you notes (Step 7).

8. Planning your finances (Step 2).

Do not get distracted from your search. Well-meaning friends and worthy charitable organizations can provide plenty of busywork to derail you from your mission. A friend once offered me a job tutoring his daughter in math so I could make a little money during my downtime. While his offer was well intentioned, it didn't align with my goal of securing a job. Because my friend was a successful consultant, I approached him later about a consulting post I'd been offered as a stepping-stone to a lucrative position; he was remarkably insightful. This showed me that people want to help but often don't know how. You have to tell them.

To stay on track, schedule your weekly activities on a calendar. Include networking events and meetings, interviews, follow-ups, and research, typically done on the web. Allow time to do things for yourself, like exercise, and fulfill obligations such as childcare. But whatever you do, always schedule eight or nine hours a day for your job search. Filling your calendar will be difficult initially. For the first few weeks, you may have only enough activities to keep you busy four or five hours a day. But keep at it and you'll soon have a packed week. This is when the job search becomes full of possibilities.

In making out your schedule, consider your own daily rhythms. When are you at your best in front of people? When's your optimum time to do research—first thing in the morning or late at night? I discovered I was a morning person, so I preferred doing interpersonal work as early in the day as possible. I'd set up my networking meetings and interviews for the first part of the day then do my research in the afternoon or evening. Mixing things up adds variety to your day and is extremely practical. For example, doing research in the afternoon allowed me to follow up on my morning interviews. We'll talk more about this in the Follow Up section.

Manage Your Money

The next item in getting organized is financial logistics. To keep focused on your job search, you must have a financial plan. Without one, you'll become distracted. This section will help you identify what you need and how to plan for it. For those of us who've managed our finances by occasionally withdrawing money with an ATM card, this will be a new discipline.

Let's start with your cash outflow. How many months of cash have you saved? If you've never considered this before and don't have a rainy-day fund, you need to put something together now. You must know how many months you can reasonably manage without a job. To determine this, divide the amount of money you have on hand by the amount you spend each month. I call this quotient the "Number." As you might imagine, once you identify it, your sense of urgency will rise. Don't panic. Your anxiety is natural. To lower it, simply manage to the Number. Here's how:

1. Now that you're not working, find ways to reduce your monthly expenditures. Examine your bank statements for the past three or four months, and calculate your average monthly expenses. Identify things you can do without or that you can delay buying. If you're the head of a family, the trick is to reduce spending without causing a household catastrophe. If you were planning a vacation, don't cancel it, but reduce it by a third.

That planned addition to your home? Postpone it until you land a new job. What about new clothes, braces for the children, and similar items?

The first time I found myself jobless, my wife and I explained to the kids, ages six to ten, that they had to do without for a while. It was difficult for them, but they managed to get by without new clothes and with less entertainment. Also, we held off purchasing a dog we had promised them. For me, the spending reductions were a little more extreme because I felt that, as head of household, I had to go without while trying to minimize the impact of my job loss on the family. So I eliminated everything possible to reduce our monthly expenses. I scheduled networking meetings over coffee instead of lunch. When our car broke down beyond repair, I took public transportation rather than buy a new one. And I put on hold little things like golfing with my buddies. The goal was to give myself leverage by reducing our monthly expenditures in a reasonable way. I recommend you do the same.

1. What sources of readily available cash do you have? For peace of mind, you'll need a stockpile before beginning your search. Consider the following sources:

    a. *Severance package.* Negotiate for one if you're let go.

    b. *401(K) and IRA.* Yes, the tax penalties for early withdrawal can be stiff, but you have to weigh the alternatives. I'm not a tax or stock advisor, but I moved all my assets into cash so they were accessible if I needed them. As it turned out, I didn't need to use them.

c. *Savings.* Inventory your savings account.

d. *Stocks and bonds.* Account for assets like these, which can be converted into cash should the need arise. Again, I'm a fan of predictable, readily available assets. Anything can happen in the short term, and if it's for the worse, you want a buffer. Do you know why the house always wins in Las Vegas? I suppose there are many reasons, but one often cited is that the house has nearly infinite resources, while you don't. If it has a bad streak, it'll recover. If you do, and you go over your threshold, you're done, and the house makes out. The same principle applies to a job search, so give yourself as much breathing room as possible to "beat the house."

e. *Relatives.* You must be careful borrowing from relatives, but if you take a small loan, agree to pay interest, and put it all in writing for a win-win situation. If Grandma's retirement fund isn't knocking it out of the park in the stock market these days, giving you a loan at interest might help her make a little money while providing you with some latitude.

f. *Doing consulting work.* Do you have any marketable skills you can parlay into consulting? This would have multiple advantages. Consulting can create income to raise your Number; provide work to boost your mental state; present networking opportunities (which we'll discuss later); and, perhaps most

> interesting of all, it can lead to a permanent position by serving as a sort of try-and-buy for both parties.

I recall the CEO of a small company interviewing me for a VP position. He was having difficulty finding a candidate with the right skill set, and clearly, I could address his needs. The organization, however, was an early stage start-up, so I was unsure of its stability. Additionally, the CEO had to get the support of several other executives as well as the company's board; given everyone's travel schedules, this would take time. He suggested a consulting arrangement that would allow him to bring me aboard almost immediately. I could start earning again and everyone could become acquainted. Perfect. So perfect, in fact, that with a newfound confidence resulting from this opportunity, I closed on a permanent job elsewhere later that week. Of course, I immediately contacted the CEO of the small company and thanked him for giving me the opportunity.

Get a Coach

A final thought on becoming organized: get yourself a coach. That's someone who can listen to your concerns, help review your progress, and provide an unbiased perspective. If you're released from a company that provides coaching as part of its outplacement services, take advantage of it. Professional career placement coaches have dealt with various situations and can provide valuable insights into your search. But they cannot run it for you, so by all means continue reading this book.

Your coach does not have to be a professional. I have one who's mentored me for many years, giving things to me straight even if they sting. Think of a coach with whom you can discuss your search every week or two. This person may be a spouse, family member, or friend who knows you well, will enjoy your successes, and can provide valuable feedback.

STEP 3: USE THE WEB AS A RESEARCH TOOL

The next few steps will help you create a foundation for pursuing your dream job. Forming this base will entail research. These techniques will aid in targeting specific companies, and we suggest procedures for networking.

What's the best way to research companies on the web? While many fee-based services are available, I've used the following free resources with great success:

Yahoo Finance. This site provides news as well as executive names and salaries. It also supplies in-depth financials, so if you want to join a growth company, you can move quickly past an organization whose previous four quarters have yielded flat revenues or declining profits. Openings at that company may be due to employee turnover. Also at Yahoo Finance, if a company is publicly traded, you can learn about its competition.

The site also provides press and analysts' comments and gives you a sense of what industry leaders think of a company.

Several websites cite employees' comments. One of the most popular, Glassdoor, provides remarks and ratings from thousands of employees.

Company websites. This resource is a natural. Key sections you should review are:

a. *Executive team.* What are members' backgrounds? This will clue you in to the company's culture, particularly if two or more executives previously worked for the same company. Executives frequently bring the culture and best practices of their former organizations to their new home.

b. *Recent earnings report.* Public companies generally cite their most recent quarterly earnings on their websites. You can also get the transcript from a quarterly earnings call to financial analysts. While reviewing the scripted comments of the CEO and CFO is worthwhile, my favorite part of these calls is the Q&A at the end. This indicates what the financial industry thinks about a company.

c. *Press releases.* Hopefully, the company has good news about new customers, breakthrough products, and financial growth. While organizations rarely promote bad news, if a press release comes across as listless or defensive, that says something, too.

d. *Products and services.* Are they easy to understand and clearly differentiated? If your area of expertise doesn't strongly align with the target company, you won't be able to analyze its products. But you can get a sense of how they're differentiated in the market.

e. *Customers.* A company that can't get customers to speak on its behalf may as well wave a red flag. If an organization does highlight its customers, look at who they are, particularly if you're in an outward-facing environment such as sales, service, marketing, or some outward aspect of engineering. Are these customers part of industries you enjoy? A colleague once told me, "When you can't enjoy having a beer with your customers, it's time to move to a new business." Great advice.

Social Networking. This has become a regular form of rapid mass communication. In the business world, the bible of social networking is LinkedIn. Others have their place, but for job searching, LinkedIn is difficult to beat.

The service provides information and connections to use in your search and to expand your network. After initial contact, you can reach out, link to a connection, and stay in touch. Your expanded network will allow you to acquire information and more contacts. You can search by name, title, company, or industry. Another virtue of LinkedIn is that you don't need a user's manual to get started.

You can Google LinkedIn to find many best practices for using the service. Here are eight of my own:

1. When you link to someone, write a personalized note. Nothing turns me off more than getting a stock LinkedIn introduction from someone I've just met. That standard intro accompanying

a request to link up is a surefire way to make a negative impression on me. I may accept the invitation, but that first negative impression will remain. Conversely, someone who takes the time to write a personalized note will stand out in my mind.

Keep the note simple. Something like, "Sarah, it was great to meet you at the marketing social last night. I enjoyed learning about your trip to Australia, as I've always wanted to visit. I hope to stay in touch." With this approach, you'll get a new connection that will serve you for a long time.

2. Give help; get help. When you receive a request for help from a respected LinkedIn contact — or from anyone in your network, for that matter — go out of your way to provide it. If the request comes in the form of a question, and you don't have an answer, think of someone in your network who might be a resource for the contact, and offer to make a connection.

3. While it's tempting to settle for the free version of LinkedIn, get the premium service. It's $30 a month and, as part of your job search, tax deductible. For this price, you'll receive three added values.

    a. *More contacts per search.* If you're searching for an executive at a given company, LinkedIn will provide up to 300 names. Review every one of them. You'll often find yourself branching into interesting new areas that can lead to additional opportunities.

b. *Anonymity while searching others.* Imagine you're probing into someone's background on LinkedIn the day before an interview, and the individual gets a notice that you've been checking up on him or her. That might seem a little creepy. With the paid service, you remain anonymous.

c. *Inmails to use in reaching out to new contacts.* As you find additional connections, you may feel awkward or intrusive asking these people to be your new "friend." But a simple inmail introducing yourself, accompanied by a well-crafted request for help, can put you at ease and prove effective.

4. It's difficult to tell if a web job posting is for a real opportunity or is part of a company requirement—but you can be sure a LinkedIn posting is valid. That's because hiring managers must pay to post jobs with LinkedIn, which indicates they've exhausted all the options within their own companies and networks (see Figure 1). They need qualified candidates and are now willing to talk with strangers—possibly including you.

You must remember, though, that the Internet creates a "low-friction" system. Literally thousands of people respond to opportunities posted on LinkedIn. Your job is to cut through the clutter. How? By identifying your contacts within the company to help you meet the hiring manager.

As a job seeker, you must connect with the hiring manager, not human resources or recruiting, which is there to filter candidates by looking for people who match or exceed a specification. HR and recruiting are chartered to present a host of candidates from which the hiring manager may choose. It's possible to succeed working through HR, but your "hit" rate will be lower. Your best bet is to find the hiring manager. The next two steps will illustrate how.

5. Once you find a job posted on LinkedIn, check for contacts. Search the company to see whom you know. This is where some level of paid LinkedIn will come in handy. The fee service will give you more contacts than the free option.

6. When you find a contact, do not send a connection. It's too invasive. As suggested in best practice 3c above, send an inmail. Explain what you need, and ask for an appointment to conduct an informational interview over the phone. Frequently, the contact will agree to connect. If you get no response, try again. You'll be amazed at how many people are willing to help others via the web. (We'll cover how to conduct the informational interview in the networking section.)

   After the interview, flatter the contact by requesting to connect on LinkedIn. Remember best practice 1 above. Send a personal note, not the standard request. Example: Ed, thanks for the help today. I enjoyed reconnecting with you. Would love to stay in touch.

7. While you're on LinkedIn, pick a few companies off your target list, see who you know among their employees, and pursue them for a networking meeting.

8. Check out who's viewed your profile—while there are various levels of access and security, you have greater visibility as to who has viewed your profile with the paid version of LinkedIn. Once I noticed that a well-known recruiter had viewed mine. When I didn't get a call, I reached out to her. As it turned out, she was searching for a job candidate but didn't think my background fit the position. I convinced her otherwise.

You can use web research to assess what job you'd like to do, learn about various industries, identify potential companies, and prepare for networking meetings. We cover these areas in subsequent steps.

STEP 4: ASSESS YOURSELF—
WHAT DO YOU REALLY WANT TO DO?

You've spent time coping with your new "career free-dom," done some initial research, and gotten yourself organized. Now it's time to develop a plan to land your next job.

This is an excellent time to evaluate your passions and determine how they can work into your career. While working full-time, you likely had little oppor-tunity to do this. Now that you've got the time, begin with the classic career-development question, what do you want to be doing in five years? That ques-tion is often difficult to answer. Some people know exactly what they want to be doing. Others are con-sidering multiple options. Some are so buried in work, family, and personal pursuits that they don't have an answer, or they know they'd be happy doing the same thing in five years. Don't let yourself get caught in this third category. My dad taught me years ago that you either grow or shrink, but you never stay the same. Even if you're doing the same job in five years, industry and technology trends will turn it into something different. To stay current, you must acquire additional skills.

The, what do you want to be doing? question applies to industries as well as vocations. Maybe you're inter-ested in a new field. If you're in networking, how do you get into storage or the Internet? If you're in IT, how do you get into sales or marketing?

So, how do you determine what you want to be doing in five years? Accomplish this in several ways:

1. Take a values-assessment test. This is a formal means of appraising your strengths and desires and mapping them to a career. Such a test is more applicable early on, when you don't have much experience or a network. Myers-Briggs, which has been around for years, assesses your preferences broadly for the kind of work you may want to do. Other tests, such as values-clarification tests, are more vocationally specific. I took one of these in high school. I wasn't sure why, or for whom, my values needed clarifying, but I took the test anyway. Three of the six vocations chosen for me were rabbi, minister, and priest; I wouldn't even begin to consider any of these. I was starting to seriously question this process when I saw, way at the bottom of the test, salesman. This vocation resonated with me for some reason, so I spent time with my guidance counselor to better understand which of my strengths correlated with being a salesman. Four years later, in my senior year at Duke University, I became a salesperson at Hewlett-Packard.

2. Read, read, read, and then read some more. The *Wall Street Journal*, *Businessweek*, Yahoo Finance, and other news sources will give you a broad sense of what's going on in the business world. Find areas that draw your attention, and explore them further.

3. Pick up an assignment that lets you delve into a new area. Whether employed with a company or not, I often took a night job or special assignment that would let me leverage my strengths and explore a new opportunity. While in marketing, I wanted to investigate product management. I approached the company's head of product management and asked if I could take on some additional projects for him. As I developed new skills, I received more latitude in my original job to perform product-management tasks. Sometime later, I left the company to lead product management for a billion-dollar organization. If you build the skills, you'll find a role requiring them.

4. Talk to contacts in your network about areas that interest you. You can even cold-call people outside the network and get amazing results. LinkedIn is a useful tool for finding people who are doing interesting things. My daughter was a design major in college. To extend her network, she became involved in the campus design community. Her involvement included volunteering to host open-house events through the department. This provided extensive exposure to campus alumni, who offered loads of insights into her major and suggested opportunities for her to consider. Ironically, one alumnus hired my daughter to start immediately after graduation. This was an impressive accomplishment, considering that when others in her department left the university, none of them had landed a job related to their vocation.

Once you've decided where you want to be in five years, what's the next step?

At least for the time being, you may have given yourself more than one possible five-year choice. If that's the case, your next step is to broaden your horizons. You're more likely to do this at a small company than a large one, because at smaller firms, people take on broader responsibilities, whereas at larger companies, they get specific assignments. On the other hand, if it's early in your career, say within the first three years of graduation from college, many large companies will create assignments that allow you to rotate throughout the organization to develop broader exposure.

Don't worry about having the perfect plan. The objective at this point is to *have* a plan. You can modify it as you network and do interviews. You'll test things, receive feedback — whether you want it or not — and evaluate what fits for you. But at the start, do have a plan.

Company Profile Preferences

Think about the ideal place to work. What are its attributes? Here are major categories to consider and some of the trade-offs. Identify what areas you're excited about, which ones you can tolerate, and which ones are deal breakers.

1. **Size of company.** Early in your career, starting with a large company can be advantageous. My

experience at Hewlett-Packard was excellent. I learned loads about how companies functioned, and I gained exposure to field sales, customer service, finance, and other operations. Consider these points regarding company size:

a. *Large company.* Big organizations once provided security but not today. Layoffs are commonplace in large companies and often not based on an employee's skill or performance. The upside is that such organizations offer a broad array of services and benefits. They generally pay well, and if a company is a market leader in a thriving market, your career path will experience fewer bumps.

b. *Start-up.* This is for the adventurous. While Google, Facebook, Apple, GE, and Walmart were all start-ups at one time, you've not heard of many others, because they failed. Many people would say that because a beginning organization is so results-oriented, its atmosphere is less political than an established company's is. Making an impact and enjoying the rush at a successful start-up can be exhilarating, but before joining one, determine where you're at in your career. Start-ups pay less because they generally offer employees a chance for big financial gains through stock, also called equity. When you join such a company, you frequently receive a large chunk of stock at a low price, and if the firm goes public or is acquired, your payout is substantial. Not all start-ups begin with equal footing, though. Venture capitalists back some of them, allowing those start-ups to pay a reasonable salary. Many have what I call "proven revenue" and pose less of a risk. Others are early stage start-ups that need a team to build out their product or service. Many of these have no funding and often pay in sweat equity. I suggest that if you're going into business with friends or people you've enjoyed working with in the past, consider the satisfaction you'll enjoy in such an environment. Otherwise, hold out for the right opportunity. In either case, a start-up poses a risk. It may not gain initial momentum, or if it has proven revenue, it may not get to the next level. If you can afford the risk and the idea is exciting to you, you should explore a start-up.

c. *Midsize company.* This organization is more established than a start-up and more flexible than a large company is. Generally, a single product has driven its expansion. The organization is often public and considered to have growth potential. It doesn't offer the extreme equity upside of a start-up, but it often provides opportunity for growth. Many people consider the midsize company a perfect blend of start-up and large organization.

2. **Company culture.** This factor is difficult to quantify and is often linked to company size. Some questions to ask:

a. Is the company amiable or aggressive?

b. Does it focus on results or relationships? (Some folks call the latter politics, but it's really about whether relationships or performance impact decisions.)

c. Which functions reflect the company's personality: Marketing? Engineering? Sales?

Unless the organization is large and well known, its culture may be difficult to ascertain at the outset. If you don't know what the culture is like, don't worry about it.

3. **Headquarters vs. field office.** If you're in high-tech and live in Silicon Valley, or if you're in retail and live in Dallas, you'll have plenty of options regarding this consideration. Field offices are generally small and have sales-oriented environments. Everyone knows everyone at the company party. But the work offers less variety and fewer opportunities for promotion. Headquarters also applies to a division of a large company. Many divisions function like midsize companies, complete with various departments, such as finance, marketing, and operations. Think about this particular move. If the personal strengths assessment mentioned above indicates you're a headquarters-marketing person, the decision has been made for you. But keep in mind that once you choose, you can make a change later in life.

4. **Location of headquarters.** After several years with Silicon Valley companies, I considered working for organizations that had a presence in the area but didn't have headquarters there. I was particularly drawn to companies based in the northeast. EMC, located in the Boston area, turned out to be actively seeking Silicon Valley

executives. The culture there was different, and I'd always enjoyed a variety of experiences when meeting with my New England counterparts. Some people enjoy working for an international company. I did this once in my career and, as a result, became more aware of world events and learned some best practices that I maintain to this day.

5. **Market position.** Do you want to work for a market leader or a market challenger? Both have their advantages. A market leader is frequently a larger company, building its products, processes, and sales around servicing existing customers and developing product extensions. Some market leaders use acquisitions to extend their reach. Cross-functional work and team building are hallmarks at these companies. My dad worked at GE for many years when Jack Welch was at the helm. Welch became known as "Neutron Jack" because if a division wasn't first or second in its field, he might sell it off or shut it down. GE grew exponentially under Jack Welch because he focused on being a market leader. Now retired, he's one of the most respected speakers and public personalities in America.

Market challengers focus more on innovation and results than on teams and processes. Their goals are to grab market share from leaders. When they succeed, company atmospheres energize. Besting a leader isn't easy, however. While environments at market challengers are often exhilarating, these companies generally demand hard work and long hours.

6. **Growth.** How important is this to you? I once decided to work for growth companies only. This strategy has its advantages: financial gain, advancement opportunities, and plenty of celebrating successes. But growth organizations have a potential downside. Because of their successes, employees sometimes feel entitled to more financial gain and advancement opportunities. This often leads to classic office politics. Additionally, when growth companies have one or two bad quarters, their cultures may not adapt readily to the changed atmospheres.

7. **Commute.** If your target companies are located a distance from your residence, you should assess your willingness to commute. Obviously, the more desirable the job, the farther you'll be willing to commute. But, to be realistic, you should establish a travel boundary; that is, the farthest you'd be willing to travel to work. The commute will then become one of several factors in your decision, as opposed to the overriding one.

Choosing an Industry

In addition to the type of company you want to pursue, you'll need to choose an industry. Select one that holds your interest and that you know something about. Industry knowledge, or domain expertise, has become increasingly important to companies, even in traditional staff functions such as finance or HR. Years ago, an organization would seek to fill and opening and recruit a "baseball player." Today, they seek a third baseman who can hit left-handed, throw right-handed, steal fifty bases a season, and bat at least .300. This may be slightly exaggerated, but you get the picture. Look for industries in which you have some domain expertise.

By evaluating your level of expertise, you can gauge how many companies will be available to you in each industry. For example, in the high-tech field, following are five levels of increasing specificity:

High-Tech

Software

Web 2.0 Applications

Social Media

Social Media for the Enterprise

Figure 3.

Item 1 applies to perhaps 5,000 companies; item 5 to fewer than fifty. You have a fair amount of flexibility early in the process. You merely want to create guidelines for your initial list of target companies. I advise people in doubt to go broad and create a longer list. You can refine it as you receive feedback from networks and interviews.

If you're not a recent college graduate, consider what you've been doing for the past five to ten years. What has captured your interest? How can you best leverage your domain expertise into the same or similar industries? What areas are providing growth and new jobs?

During my ten years at Hewlett-Packard, I worked with classic high-tech systems products, exposing me to a number of related industries — engineering design software, networking, and storage, which I explored later in my career.

What about changing industries? If you're considering it, ask yourself why. If the new industry maps well into your preferences from the section above, then consider it a possible choice. But notice I said possible. Early in the search, you want to keep your options open. You *will* get feedback.

If you choose to change industries, you'll need a strong sponsor — someone who will benefit from your joining the company. A sponsor typically has had a prior relationship with you or been introduced to you through a network. This individual will be required to attest to your "soft skills" and "chemistry" to get you in the door. Your sponsor will benefit from having an ally within the company. While finding a sponsor requires work, there's no way around it. In a world in which companies no longer hire baseball players, you need help to overcome your lack of expertise in certain areas. We explore in the networking section how to reach out to people and get that sponsor.

**Tie it Together—
Create a List of Target Companies**

Now that you've listed your preferences and assessed your target industries, you're ready to create a list of companies to target. A target list will give you a platform for networking. When you group companies on the list by industry, you'll find related organizations to talk to, thereby expanding your list. In addition, a target list will help you keep track of your own preferences. You'll see which industries you're adding companies to and which you're subtracting from — in other words, which industry lists are expanding and which are contracting. This will accelerate your progress by further helping you identify the best industries to target.

Here's how to build your list of target companies:

Up to this point in Step 4, we have covered the type of job you want to do, the kind of company you want to work for, and the industries you want to be part of. To start the target company list, focus on industries. On a blank sheet of paper, list local companies you'd be interested in working for within the target industries. We're not talking about positions yet, just companies. You want to finish with a list of fifty to one hundred organizations you'd be happy with. If you can't come up with a number within that range, check out the web or local chamber of commerce to get a better idea of who's around. Not all companies need headquarters in your area. For example, you can put Google on your list, even if you don't live in Silicon Valley. After all, the company has branch offices and divisions around the world.

Now that you have an initial list of companies to target, you can refine it. Look at your homework regarding company and job type at the beginning of Step 4. Use those criteria to eliminate organizations that don't make sense now. For example, if you have a list of ten companies in a particular industry but decide you want to focus only on large organizations, eliminate all the small and midsize companies on the list. This refinement won't be extensive, but your list of target organizations will give you a road map for your networking meetings. At this point, you'll have reduced the list to thirty to fifty companies. Your criteria and list likely will change as you learn more. After a month or two of networking and refining, you'll have a manageable list of twenty to thirty companies.

Remember the research papers you did in high school? If you listened to your teachers, you created an outline then wrote several drafts. You edited each, thereby improving the paper as you went along. Rarely did you do your best work on the first draft— well, some students claimed they did, but I always doubted it. The same principle applies to conducting research while seeking a job. You need an initial plan based on your assumptions, but as you collect data through networking and interviewing, you'll edit your draft as you learn more about what you really want.

Use the criteria from company and job type to refine your list. The refinement will be slight at this stage of the process, probably 10 percent or less. But now you have a working list of companies. To make the list more complete and easier to read, add information about each company, formatted as in Figure 4.

Figure 4.

Job Search list for Ellen Searcher　　　　**April 26, 2012**

Industry: industry 1

Company name	*Potential position*	*Hiring manager/title*
ABC Company*	Sales Representative	Don Big/Sales Mgr.
DEF Company	Account Manager	Bill Tip/Sales Mgr.
GHI Company	Sales Representative	Carol Jones/VP of Sales

Industry: industry 2

JKL Company*	Inside Sales	Jack Tan/Sales Dir.
MNO Company	Account Manager	Doug Trout/VP of Sales

To start with, type the companies' names, grouped by industry, in a column on the left side of the page, spelling the names correctly. Identify whether each entry is a headquarters, division, or branch office of the company to ensure your networker has all potentially helpful information.

Place an asterisk next to the name of any company at which you have some momentum, either through an interview, a discussion with a recruiter, or a good contact. I refer to these as opportunities "in play." Focus on them, especially early in your search. Momentum is a wonderful thing, and you're looking for ways to create it. Your asterisks will progress nicely, and while they may not always end in job offers, they'll give you early feedback on your plan.

Your asterisks will also be useful in the next step: networking. People love to help people who have gained momentum, but they're reluctant to jump into the boat of an unknown quantity, namely "you without a job." Your asterisks will validate you heading into your network meetings.

Next on your job-search list is identifying the position you want to pursue at each company. You may have several posts in mind, particularly early in your search when you're looking at a broad cross section of companies. My goal was VP of marketing for a medium to large organization. If there were several positions of this sort at the larger companies, I'd narrow my focus to VP of product marketing. At smaller companies, the position was always CMO. The message: align the position you're seeking with the target company.

You *must* be specific. I was once approached by a good friend looking for a job. When I asked him what companies he was targeting, he said he had none. When I asked what position he was interested in, he said, rather vaguely, marketing, operations, and engineering. He found a job but eventually was laid off and never regained his footing. This may have been because he was as vague during his interviews as he was with me.

Each entry on your list should include the name of the target manager, if you can get it. This will become easier the higher you climb in your career. If you're pursuing an engineering vice president job at a mid-size company, you'll have only one senior vice president of engineering or several SVP/GM types to look for, and they likely will be listed on the company's website. For managers who aren't so obvious, you can research a good business-networking site like LinkedIn to determine your target. For example if you're in sales, start with the head of sales on the executive team. If you're pursuing an entry-level job at a large company, someone as high-level as head of sales may not be a reasonable target. Refine your search by doing a little profiling on LinkedIn. For a salesperson living in Philadelphia, look up: company name, sales manager, Philadelphia. When in doubt, list the highest-level contact you feel is reasonable. If all you have is the EVP of worldwide sales, list him or her. It will help if you're networking with another high-level executive who hangs around people at this level.

Keep this list on your computer, and update it every week or two. When you remove a company, place it in an appendix or section labeled "removed" in the back so you have a record of the companies you're no longer pursuing. As you go through the process, you'll be amazed at the changes in your list. Just for fun, compare two lists one month apart. Notice the difference? If you've done the work, you will. The change is a sign that you're learning and getting closer to your ideal targets.

Keeping weekly records has another advantage. By tracking companies you've removed from the list, you'll avoid pursuing an undesirable company twice. This will give you a significant productivity advantage over competition looking for similar jobs.

Your job-search list will be a critical tool in the networking part of the process, so you need to think through this exercise carefully. Do not force network-ers to think too hard. Be specific, and help them tar-get contacts where you have strength. Some feel this approach is too limiting, but an old saying applies here: "If you don't know where you want to go, any path will get you there." If you're specific and direct, your networkers may have related ideas they'll be glad to share. During my networking meetings, when I listed Symantec, a major security-software player, people usually came up with names from Cisco, McAfee Software, and IBM.

Manage Your Progress with a Funnel

Once you create a list of target companies—a snap-shot of organizations you want to pursue—you have an essential tool for conducting your networking meeting (Step 5 covers the meeting itself). You'll track your progress with companies you've engaged via yet another tool, the "funnel," which you'll update after each networking meeting and interview.

Most people in sales are familiar with the funnel concept.

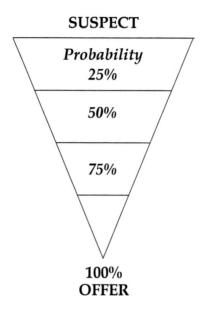

Figure 5.

Each funnel cross section shows your opportunities as they progress. A 10 percent probability this week may become 25 percent next week and 50 percent two weeks from now. The opportunity may progress to an offer or fall out of the funnel at some point. What you're doing is organizing all those opportunities to create a picture of where they are.

Think of pouring liquid into an actual funnel. As you pour, pressure from the new liquid forces down the mass already in the funnel. Similarly, new opportunities "poured" into your funnel create pressure and momentum for your search. Your goal is to force the 50 and 75 percent probability opportunities into an offer. These are your hot prospects with the best chance of concluding your search. Pay attention to other opportunities, but focus mainly on these.

Research shows they'll move more naturally from "suspect," the earliest stage of the process, to an offer.

How do you assign a probability to each entry in your funnel? I have a formula that uses two measures for each opportunity.

First is your position relative to the competition in your search. If through a strong network contact, someone has introduced you to a hiring manager who hasn't posted an opening and your skills fit the manager's needs, you're essentially unchallenged in your efforts. This is an ideal situation, and it should rate 100 percent as a competition measure. If you are one of many candidates, if you have a loose connection through your network, and if you are working hard simply to get the initial interview, you're fighting to compete and not to win. In this case, your competitive measure would not be as great.

The second measure is the likelihood the company will hire. In the scenario above, in which you're competing unchallenged, your chances of getting an offer are much better if the hiring manager has a hiring budget and plans to create a position. The chances are far poorer if there's no hiring budget, no plans to fund an opening, and the company is tightening its belt because of slower growth.

Here's how to weigh various common scenarios for the two measures:

PERCENT PROBABILITY	COMPETITION	LIKELY TO HIRE
Suspect	Unknown	Unknown
25%	Many	Budgeted
50%	One Other Finalist	Posted
75%	Present But Trails	Discussing Offer
100%	Nonexistent	Discussing Offer

Figure 6.

Let's add more detail to each of the categories above, and then calculate the entry for your funnel. A suspect is a company you'd like to pursue. You may have heard that it's hiring. You've researched the organization on the web and seen good growth. Or someone you know has recently joined the company and can help you. Not all targets are suspects. Your research data merely suggest that these organizations may represent opportunities for you.

A 25 percent competitive measure means the competition is dominant, or many competitors are after the same job. The hiring manager views you as one of these candidates but has little to distinguish you from the others. A 25 percent measure means a position is budgeted, usually for the next one or two quarters. Although the company hasn't fully committed to the hire yet, this is a positive position to have when you enlist your network to help you. Remember the concentric circles we covered at the beginning of this book? You want to be in the first two circles before a feeding frenzy begins, and you face enormous competition.

At 50 percent for either measure, you are making real progress. For the competitive measure, you're one of two candidates that company is considering for the job. You likely have met with several decision makers and you're clearly a fit. Keep in mind, however, that the company must still commit to funding the position. Business may slow, an acquisition rumor may surface, or a hiring manager may be released, and the opening might disappear. A 50 percent measure means the job is posted. Now you can see why so many postings are meaningless. If one or more candidates, internal or external, have been networking well, they've probably met with the hiring manager and gone through the interview process before you've even seen the posting. This doesn't always happen, but it happens so often that most career counselors advise ignoring job postings.

At 75 percent both measures are well under way in your favor. You're the chosen candidate, and the job is yours to lose. Some people with this measurement do lose out because of an unfavorable circumstance, but such cases are rare. More likely you're working with a hiring manager, or even human resources, to develop an offer letter for you to join the company.

A 100 percent competitive measurement does not necessarily mean that you've received an offer letter, but rather you're the only candidate. As we discussed earlier, this frequently happens when you get a strong sponsor early in the process and are an excellent fit with the hiring manager. The lucky manager has found a solution to his or her problem and has probably moved on to other matters. From a likely-to-hire perspective, 100 percent probably signals an offer letter has been agreed to and is now moving through human resources. I suppose this really is a 98 to 99 percent measurement, but most companies recognize the value of integrity, and once they've committed to you orally, they'll rarely rescind an offer, even in the face of a business downturn.

Now that you've identified the probabilities for the competition and likely-to-hire measures, let's discuss the formula to determine where you're at in the hiring process and your probability of getting a particular opportunity. Treat the competition and likely-to-hire measures independently. Analyze where you are with each one from the descriptions above. Multiply them together to get your funnel entry. If your competitive and likely-to-hire measures are each 25 percent, your overall funnel entry is .25 x .25, or about 6 percent. (I round up to 10 percent to make it easy.) If your competitive measure is 100 percent and your likely-to-hire measure is 50 percent, your overall funnel entry is 50 percent. By applying these measures, you'll have a less subjective funnel. And you'll discover what salespeople have known for years: funnel management is a science. The greater your total probabilities, the greater the chance you'll land a job.

When completed, the funnel will be a chart that I call an "Opportunity Report" and looks like this:

Company	Position	Next Steps
75% ABC Corp.	Chief Mkting Officer (CMO)	Awaiting offer week of 12/17
50% DEF Company	CMO	Met with/3 exec's 12/5 Awaiting next steps for week of 12/17
25% GHI Company JKL Company MNO Corp.	VP/SVP Strategy VP Solutions VP/SVP Mkting	Pinged CEO 12/6. No response. Try in Jan. 12/19 meeting with CMO delayed until Jan. 11/29, heard back from CEO. On hold. Drop to 25%.
10% PQR Corp.	CMO	12/7, good meeting w/recruiter. Meet with CEO in new year.
SUSPECTS STU Company	CMO	They started a search then dropped it. Keep on radar.
DROPPED VWX Corp.	SVP Products	Heard from Executive VP. Company picked other finalist.

Figure 7.

You've listed each company according to its probability that you have calculated using the formula above. You've identified each position and have documented the next steps for you to easily track.

The target list and funnel are the two tools you'll use to monitor your job search. The list will show you where to go, while the funnel will serve as your navigation system. Just as the financial community uses both the balance sheet and income statement to provide different views of a company's health, the target list and funnel will offer a snapshot of your search's health. Update them frequently, perhaps Monday mornings before you start your workday. You'll find that as you progress in making all those new entries and updates, you'll derive a wonderful sense of accomplishment.

You may want to share these two documents with people who can help in your search efforts. The funnel is an excellent tool to show your coach (see Getting Organized section). The snapshot will give this individual an excellent overview and serve as the basis for a conversation about your progress. In the next section on networking, we cover how to use your target list to turn your networking meetings into real opportunities for growing your funnel.

STEP 5: CREATE YOUR NETWORK BATTLE PLAN

Now that you have a target list of companies, you need to meet with people who can help you. Otherwise known as networking, this is the single most difficult part of a job search. Many of us are uncomfortable asking others for help. This is especially true if we don't know those others well—or at all. But by following the process described in this chapter, you'll find yourself reaching out to all sorts of people—and with confidence at that.

In the beginning of this book, Figure 1 depicted the networked world of the hiring manager. Figure 8 shows your networked world. Compile an initial networking list. Since you're not used to talking to others about a job search, start with people you know well, such as family, close friends, mentors, former bosses, or customers; they'll be less threatening. These members of your inner circle are people you can confide in, who can tell if you're feeling insecure about your search, and who will coach you. If you make a few mistakes in these early conversations, no problem. Perhaps you're still refining your job-hunting story and fine-tuning what you want to do and what you have to offer. Your inner circle is a good place to perfect your conversation. Former coworkers are unlikely to be on this initial list, unless they've been extremely successful since you worked together.

Often, former colleagues revel a little in others' misfortune. They can be part of your network eventually, but not at this stage of the process.

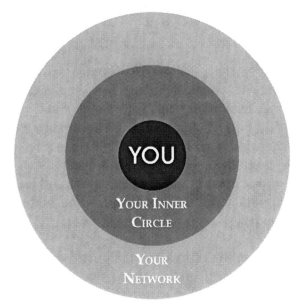

Figure 8.

The next group of people to meet with is your classic network. You may think you don't have one, but you'd be surprised. Examine your LinkedIn list if you have one. If you don't, draw up a list of people you have spoken with in the past. Be as inclusive as possible. Many people on my list aren't members of my inner circle, but I know that a number of them would love to hear from me, particularly vendors I've done business with in the past. Many people like to help others in a pinch, and vendors often realize they must invest a little to get something back. At this point, former partners and coworkers would also make good contacts. Once you've got a little momentum going and have more confidence in your story, former colleagues may be excellent sources of information. And if they're enduring struggles of their own, they could even see you as a source of hope.

What about people, such as your doctor, dentist, or hair stylist? My stylist cuts hair for more Silicon Valley executives and their secretaries and golf buddies than you can imagine. He's given me many leads for jobs, people to hire, partners, and so forth. George has been happy to introduce me, and I've been thrilled to get the connection.

In my networking efforts I've approached waiters, checkout clerks, my kids' teachers — you name it. All have access to hiring managers. Someone taught me long ago that somewhere in the universe, a hiring manager is waking up in a cold sweat at 3:00 a.m. wondering where I am so he or she can hire me. My network could very well lead me to that hiring manager.

Earlier we touched on exercise. The gym can be a great place to network. People there are often like-minded professionals trying to balance work and their personal lives as well as make more connections. But don't go to the gym in the middle of the workday, when other unemployed guys hang out, often to draw pity for their plight. Go when working professionals are there — before the workday begins or after it's over, right before dinner. In other words, go when the fish are biting. While I was unemployed, my wife found it funny that I'd set the alarm for five thirty in the morning in order to arrive at the gym early. But she was also impressed when I came home with two or three job leads.

Now you've got lists of people to contact and companies to share with them. How do you approach these contacts to get their help in connecting with hiring managers on your list?

The process is simple. Explain why you're calling and what happened in your previous job (by now you've got a well-rehearsed story from Step 1). Then tell them, direct and to the point, what help you'd like.

It can go like this:

Bob: *Jim, hi, it's Bob.*

Jim: *Hey, Bob, it's been a long time. What's up?*

Bob: *Yes, I realize it's been a while, and I don't feel proud contacting you when we haven't spoken for so long, but I could use your insights on something. Last week, the company I've been with, ABC Inc., made some changes and let me go.*

Jim: *Don't worry about it. That sort of thing happens all the time. But I don't know how I can help. You're in marketing, and I'm an engineer.*

Bob: *Well, I've put together a list of twenty-five to thirty companies I'm targeting for my next move. I already have traction with some of them, and it would be great to get your thoughts on the organizations and people I'm talking to.*

Jim: Sure, I can do that.

Bob: Beer some evening after work or coffee in the morning?

Jim: Coffee next Tuesday at 7:00 a.m. I look forward to seeing you, Bob.

A few points from this dialogue to keep in mind:

1. The first portion explains the call's purpose and what happened. Once contacts acknowledge your situation, even if they seem hesitant, like Jim, tell them what insights you need.

2. The word help could be scary for contacts. Use a similar word, coaching, especially with sports-oriented men. Other options are words like insights and perspective.

3. Asking people for their insights and input on your plan is flattering.

4. Because you have a list and some traction already, you're making this easy for contacts. Remember, people will want to help you, but they won't know how, and they will not extend themselves too far until they see you as a winning ride. Later, we'll get to the actual meeting itself, and you'll be amazed at how easily contacts can provide you with names to add to your list.

If the contact is someone you don't know, or if getting together will be inconvenient because of travel or a busy schedule, respect the person's time, and make it easy to accept your request for a meeting. For example, consider reaching out via e-mail and proposing a phone call rather than a face-to-face talk. Suggest a ten to fifteen-minute conversation.

Okay, you have a meeting with someone in your network. How many such get-togethers do you need each week? Some argue more is better, but I'm not so sure. Though I went through weeks during which I had maybe ten networking meetings, if I was engaging with hiring managers on actual interviews, the number naturally declined. The important thing is to keep yourself productive for at least eight hours a day.

Here are some tips on how to prepare for a network meeting:

1. Do a quick check of the contact's background, including current title and company and recent accomplishments. You can get this information from the person who made the introduction or from LinkedIn. If the contact is from your inner circle, you probably won't have to do research.

2. On the day of the meeting, check Yahoo Finance or the website of the contact's company for recent news. Often the organization will make a major announcement that you'll want to discuss with your contact at the meeting. Get the person's take on it, and ask one or two questions to gain insights on what drove the company to act as it did.

3. Bring a clean, updated copy of your job-search list. All that work you did in the previous section

is about to pay off. This list will make it easier for your network to help you by triggering ideas for new contacts and companies.

The Networking Meeting

The day of your networking meeting has arrived. As Bob and Jim decided, a get-together over coffee or tea is the best option. It's more informal and requires less of your contact's time. Pick a local hangout but avoid Starbucks. When I was out of work, the unemployed seemed to frequent that popular coffeehouse for some reason. Spending time there with other out-of-work people, who may not be as focused as you on getting that next job, could lower your morale, to say nothing of hamper your job search.

As for how to conduct the networking meeting, I'd suggest the following flow, starting with when to arrive at the meeting:

Plan to arrive at the restaurant or coffeehouse fifteen minutes before your appointment for three reasons:

1. You do not want to be late, because that will send the wrong message.

2. Arriving early will allow you to relax, find a table, and arrange the setting.

3. It can prevent awkwardness over who should pay for whose coffee. Your contact is doing you a favor, but you're unemployed. By getting to the meeting place ahead of time, you can buy your

own coffee, thereby preventing any discomfort over the issue.

Here's how the discussion might go:

You: Jim, thanks for meeting with me today. As I mentioned over the phone, ABC Company has let me go.

Jim: Gee, that's too bad. What happened? (Even if you covered the situation over the phone, you may need to explain it again.)

You (with your story at the ready): Well, my boss resigned, and his replacement brought in his own team.

Jim: That happens all the time. How can I help you?

You: I've been thinking about companies I'd like to work for, where I can have an impact. Here's a list I've put together. You'll see that I already have interviews scheduled with four of the organizations. I'd appreciate any thoughts you might have on the list – your opinions of the companies, people who work for them that I can talk to, anyone who knows the industry, and so forth.

Jim: Let me see your list, and I'll tell you what I know.

Give Jim your list and be quiet while he reads it over and develops his thoughts. This may be easier said than done, because silence makes many of us uncomfortable. In your case, you may be feeling vulnerable because you're unemployed and asking for help, and you've just handed over a package you've put together. But remaining silent is necessary. You'll get through this moment if you keep the following in mind:

1. The silence will be the most excruciating sixty to ninety seconds you'll go through all day.

2. Despite how painful the quiet may be for you, keep in mind that it'll signify confidence. It will say, "I've prepared for this meeting, and I'm putting myself out there. You've agreed to help me with your wisdom and insights, so step up and show me what you've got, big boy."

Trust me, if you've done your homework and delivered your message with confidence, the pressure will be on Jim to deliver. Although he may be a friend, he likely came to this meeting with a hint of smugness. He's employed, you're not, and you've asked for his opinions. But now you've delivered the goods, and he must demonstrate that you weren't mistaken in considering him a worthy source of information. So be quiet, and let him read that list while formulating ideas to help you.

Jim likely will ask you about the opportunities you've got in play. Tell him how you got them from others in your network. After all, if they've delivered, certainly he can too. Note the status of each opportunity, particularly those that look like the best fit. Ask if he knows about any of them. The in-play opportunities are an appropriate place to start. Jim may know of another manager or executive at the company. He might even get a buzz helping connect you — an obvious winner — with this person.

So these in-play targets are potentially low-hanging fruit for Jim. If he doesn't offer anything up, ask him how other companies on the list strike him. He'll likely provide contacts or opinions or both. People often don't realize that a simple opinion from a trusted source is invaluable. Suppose Jim looks at DEF Company on your list and says, "I'd be careful with that one. They recently laid people off, and sales have been down for two years. Even if you get in, you may soon be looking for a job again."

Wonderful. You can now cross a flawed opportunity off your list. Let your job-searching competition waste time with DEF Company while you focus on a better target.

A mentor of mine once offered me similar advice about a company I thought I could have an impact at. He said, "Don't go there, Bob. This company isn't doing very well." Three years later, I actually met the organization's former CEO, who by then had moved on. He told me of the company's troubles, and how three years before, when the company seemed at its peak, the warning signs were there, and he became desperate to sell it. Eventually he did, at a fraction of what it was worth when I looked at it. So by warning me off, my mentor had saved me considerable misery.

Now let's consider another possible scenario. Jim knows of a key manager at one or two of your target companies. This person isn't someone you're targeting, but rather a key player, who can broker an introduction or help you keep your navigation system in place. Here's how the dialogue with Jim should go:

> **Jim:** *I see you're interested in KLM company. Tell me about that.*
>
> **You:** *Well, I worked for its competitor for four years, and I know the industry. I think I could hit the ground running as director of public relations at KLM, since I know writers at the top publications and major analysts in the industry.*
>
> **Jim:** *I see you're targeting the VP of marketing over there. I don't know him, but I'm acquainted with the sales VP. Would that help?*
>
> **You:** *It would be helpful if I could have a twenty-minute informational interview with him. I'd like to understand what issues KLM is addressing, what the VP needs from the marketing team, and how I can best position my experience to help.*
>
> **Jim:** *That sounds good. How about sending me a resume, and I'll forward it to the VP of sales.*
>
> **You:** *Actually, Jim, could I send him an e-mail introducing myself and copy you? Then he can decide what to do.*
>
> **Jim:** *Fine by me. Let's keep looking down this list.*

Some points to keep in mind from this part of the conversation:

1. Jim *will* identify someone for you to meet somewhere

    a.   At the company.

    b.   In the industry.

    c.   In his network but not within a or b.

2.   When asked about a particular entry, have a ready explanation for why this company and why this person. Always talk in terms of what you can do for the company to help it succeed. Suggest an informational interview or a session to review the lay of the land.

3.   Do not give Jim your resume to send. This would put him in an awkward position, because he'd be endorsing your resume right down to any misspellings. Moreover, although Jim means well, a person in this sort of situation typically stalls, forgets, or decides not to follow through as promised.

4.   Also, do not let Jim send an introductory e-mail — with or without your resume — to his contact. Again, though he may mean well and possibly be enjoying this moment of grandeur in which you're seeking his counsel, his priorities will quickly change when he gets back to his desk and finds five people vying for his attention. You'll become a low priority and, after not hearing from him, wonder what happened and whether you should follow up, and if so, how often. Take control, and send the e-mail yourself, referencing Jim and, if you'd like, sending him a copy. In summary, own the process.

In this conversation Jim may refer you to a recruiter. If he does, be grateful. Good people get lots of calls from recruiters. If they're happily employed, they may refer other good people to fill the position. If Jim refers you, you are, by definition, a good person.

Bear in mind that not all networking meetings will be enjoyable, let alone fruitful. A friend of mine once introduced me to a viable contact — or so he thought. Simply put, the coffee meeting was a dud. This contact was in the service business; I in marketing. Because we were in noncompeting fields, I hoped we could exchange ideas and contacts. Unfortunately, our styles clashed. While it takes me time to warm up to a new contact, he was talkative from the start, revealing details about himself as if I were an old friend. We never got down to a reasonable networking conversation. I suffered through the meeting, thanked my friend for the introduction, and erased the memory. You should too if something similar happens. Rather than let a clunker throw you, just move on down the line.

Case Study—Networking

Alex was a successful salesman with a top high-tech company. He achieved his quota regularly and was rep of the year for North America. Another organization acquired the company, however, and since many account managers overlapped as a result, the expanded organization released him along with a number of other employees.

Upon embarking on his search, he started out seeking new employment in the traditional way. He looked at job boards, talked to recruiters, and submitted his resume to the HR people at companies he wanted to work for. While there were a number of callbacks, they were only from companies with poor sales, poor profits, and poor management. Occasionally, he'd call me and describe his progress. I was amazed to see this accomplished salesperson talking to start-ups that had no track record and that typically attracted underperformers from established companies.

The top organizations were looking for high-performing salespeople who were *recommended* to them. But Alex hadn't gotten the memo. I asked whether he had any contacts at these companies. He said he did but was so focused on all his leads he didn't have time for a strategic attack. I could see the toll this was taking on him, so one day I insisted that I take control of the process, and he didn't resist.

Since Alex knew what kind of job and company he wanted, I had him focus on industries. We discussed which ones would best suit his background then identified several target companies within them. I told him to write down the names of potential hiring sales managers. Then I gave him a goal: conduct ten networking meetings the following week to identify connections within those companies. The first get-together would be with me. We identified nine other people he would meet with during the next week.

At my request, Alex brought his updated target company list to our subsequent meeting. I reviewed it and quickly identified three connections for him. I asked him what progress he'd made getting the other nine meetings set up. Not much, he said. I decided it was time to get tough. Since this ambitious professional had accepted me as his coach, I took the responsibility seriously. This was a motivated guy with a successful track record, who was losing his edge. I told him that every Friday night I wanted a spreadsheet from him listing all the networking meetings he'd scheduled and a pipeline of his interview opportunities. He would rate each of these from 10 to 75 percent after we reviewed the definition of each level. I could see the fear in his eyes. Fortunately, though, Alex was highly motivated and sent me his spreadsheet weekly. I replied with comments, and every other week we talked over the phone. After a month, Alex had several excellent opportunities, which further energized him. After two months, he'd garnered multiple opportunities that clearly were approaching offers. He ended up receiving two and now has a perfect fit with a super company and is making more money than ever.

To repeat what we said earlier, one of the best ways to make your funnel and target lists work for you is to get a coach. Among other things, this person will keep you accountable. While you may have access to outplacement services if you're part of a company layoff, most of the time you'll need to find your own coach. Ideally, this person should be someone from your inner circle. I was Alex's former boss; we'd kept in touch over the years and had helped each other on many occasions. Granted, Alex didn't request that I be his coach—I simply forced the issue.

My wife did much the same thing with me, "suggesting" I provide her with a funnel each week. Her coaching wasn't quite the same as mine with Alex, but it was pretty direct at times.

Think about whom you want as a coach. A mentor? Former boss? Bright peer in a noncompeting area? None of the above? Doesn't matter; pick *someone*.

Networking after You Land the Job

Once when I landed a job after an intensive search, I decided to let nothing distract me from focusing on the new position. Within a few weeks of joining the company, however, my boss resigned, leaving a hole that the company would clearly fill from the outside. I immediately felt at risk and in need of a contingency plan. I wanted to accomplish three things:

1. Get insights into my new role. My network included some terrific mentors, and many were eager to advise a rising executive who would listen to them.

2. Keep avenues to new roles active in case my role should change or disappear in the impending transition. I decided too many things were simply out of my control in this world, so I'd take my best shot in the role, aim for the best, and prepare for the worst.

3. Offer to reciprocate wherever I could. Many people had helped me get to this new role, and I felt a great deal of gratitude toward them. The universe does not reward a one-way street. These people

had helped me, and though they hadn't asked me to reciprocate, I wanted to make it easy for them to do so.

All three things I wanted to accomplish involved maintaining my network. But how was I to do that? For one thing, I'd send follow-up notes, individually crafted like my initial thank-yous. I'd also create a newsletter so I could stay in touch with the seventy to eighty people in my network without sending out individual messages. I took the following actions to get these things done.

First, I followed up with anyone who, in response to my note, proposed that we get together for lunch or coffee. Sure, people often don't mean it when they suggest such things, but sometimes they do — in this case, perhaps because they wanted to hear about my success and share their own. What I knew for sure was that every member of my network had a unique story to tell from his or her experience in the industry. Over the next few months, I met with people who gave me valuable information that would help me in my new role. Additionally, I bolstered my relationships with my networkers, which allowed me to easily reciprocate all they had done for me.

I'd worked for one man I'd met with (I'll call him Tim) years before. At that time he was a well-known senior leader in the marketing industry and had been written up in books, newspapers, and magazine articles. He'd gone through his own career transition while I was experiencing mine. Now less visible to the public eye, Tim was as sharp and insightful as ever. We'd met over coffee during my original job search, and after I landed my new position, he had suggested we get together for lunch. We caught each other up on our new careers, exchanged stories, and offered updates on executives we each knew from the past. Then I got around to a specific problem I wanted to run by him. The executive vice president of sales from my new company apparently was not getting the kind of help he needed from other members of the marketing team and had asked me to assist with a special project. I valued Tim's perspective on the project itself and on how to navigate the potential political landmine of becoming the "new shiny toy" on the team, thereby earning others' resentment. Sure enough, Tim provided helpful insights into how to organize the project, include others on the marketing team, and write up the team's progress so the report reflected well on all participants. I returned to work that afternoon confident I knew what to do.

I dove into the new assignment immediately upon arriving at the office. First, I created a tiger team, a temporary committee that addresses a particular project or issue. These groups are often highly visible and cross functional. I made sure that key marketing people were named to my team, as well as a couple of key managers who worked for the project's sponsor, the executive vice president of sales. After working through various issues and arriving at our conclusions, we prepared a presentation for the executive VP. I minimized my role and made sure that both sales and marketing people gave the presentation. This was about getting the needed results, not about pumping me up. The presentation came off spectacularly well, and the head of sales expressed his appreciation.

Not all of my follow-ups were with people more senior than me. A young lady (I'll call her Sheila) had been a coworker years before at Sun Microsystems. We'd reconnected a few times since, and it was always easy to pick up where we had left off. During my job search, I sought to get Sheila's take on some companies I was looking at. While she didn't have any introductions for me, she provided loads of insights. After I'd been in my role a few months, Sheila contacted me. She'd grown disenchanted with her situation at work. She faced too many deadlines, with too few resources, at a company whose revenues were declining. Sheila wanted to run some companies by me. But a surprising thing happened. Sheila told me about her current use of the social media, an area I'd considered a possible asset for my current organization. Her insights and experience with these media were incredibly valuable.

Thus, both Tim and Sheila, valuable members of my network, helped me with my first objective above, getting insights into my new role so I could ramp up quickly.

The second thing I did after following up with those who'd offered to meet with me was to maintain a spreadsheet that tracked my contacts. I kept a long list of everyone who'd helped me in the search. After sending an initial set of thank-yous, I highlighted twenty contacts on the list that I felt I had to stay in touch with. I would reach out to them quarterly via e-mail or lunch, offering to help them and updating them on my progress. I reviewed the list weekly to make sure I stayed on top of things.

One of my contacts was Joe, a high-powered consultant who'd provided me with tremendous insights into companies I was pursuing during my search. He knew the players so well that he could tell people what they'd had for breakfast the previous day. Joe had always responded to my e-mails, which was impressive considering the high demand for his company's services. Then I got a lucky break. My counterpart at another company had received an assignment that was clearly beyond her team, but rather than terminate half a dozen people, she wanted to enlist an outsider to get her program on the rails. Did I know any consultants with the needed expertise? I did. It happened to be Joe.

I called him, and he graciously agreed to meet with my counterpart. The get-together went well. She brought Joe on, and I won a few points with her. Of course, Joe was grateful for the new business. Rendering this assistance helped me fulfill objective 3 above: to reciprocate with those who'd aided me in my career.

Maintain a spreadsheet of eighty people, and keep in touch with the top twenty. As you reconnect with the other sixty in the normal course of networking—at community and industry events and the like—make a note on your spreadsheet. This will allow you to track whom you're connecting with regularly. But you can't stay in touch with all eighty people on a one-to-one basis. That's where the next idea comes in.

If you're wondering about objective 2 (keeping my irons in the fire just in case), all this work contributed to that. Yet I wanted to broaden my reach with something more. So besides maintaining my network through one-on-one relationships, I've added a little air cover. Every six months I send an e-mail newsletter to all eighty people on my list. I thank them for their help and, as humbly as I can, let them know about my accomplishments, how great things are going, and what a terrific company I've joined. Although it's a mass e-mail, I'm amazed at the responses I've received—everything from "Thanks for the note" to a lunch invitation (hey, people like hanging out with a winner). Give yourself some broad exposure, and send out your own e-mail newsletter.

Remember the three ways to stay in touch once you've landed a job:

1. Send a thank-you note to everyone who helped you. This may be as many as eighty people, many of who will suggest getting together for lunch or coffee. Do it.

2. Keep a spreadsheet of these people, and highlight the top twenty you must stay in touch with.

3. Send a biannual e-mail newsletter.

Networking at Events

Holiday parties, industry gatherings, and even your kids' sports events are all ideal networking opportunities. Attend as many of these as possible, and, while you don't want to seem as if you're working the room like a politician, meet as many people as you can. Navigating these opportunities with some grace can set you apart from the pack of other job seekers and provide you with additional avenues of networking.

Being well-read and adept at small talk (see Step 7) can help you engage in lively conversation. Chatting is best done one-on-one, but as you gain confidence, you'll be able to entertain a small crowd. At some point in any conversation, someone may ask you about your vocation. Tell your story with confidence, and then reveal what you're doing to find your next role. Mention your target list, and ask if you can connect later to get some "coaching" on your activities, including the person's slant on companies where you have interviews scheduled. Get the individual's contact information and follow up.

Let's say you're at a neighborhood get-together talking to an older man, Rick, about local schools. You haven't engaged with him before but can see he's bright and articulate. You sense that if Rick's not a working professional now, at one time he was a rocket. Ask him what he does. People love to talk about themselves, and Rick likely will tell you about his background and skills. If your hunch is correct, you'll learn if he can be an asset in your network. If that doesn't work out, well, you've had the pleasure of his company.

If you think Rick can be of help, tell him you're looking for employment, have several companies in mind, and would appreciate his slant on them. Would he mind if you called him sometime? This will get you

Rick's contact information and help you conclude the conversation on a positive note.

You'll notice that nowhere in this chat have you reviewed your target list. Diving into business at a social event is in poor taste, so always ask permission to connect later. This likely will strike people as unassuming and make it easier for them to say yes.

What if your situation doesn't come up easily as our example with Rick in these types of conversations? If you've enjoyed talking to a person, thank him or her for spending time with you and get the individual's contact information. Wait several days, a week at the most, and drop the person an e-mail. Acting too quickly could indicate you're desperate, and you don't want to scare the squirrels away with any sudden movement. In your e-mail, remind the individual who you are and how you met. Say you enjoyed the conversation, and then share your situation. Indicate you were hoping for some insights into your job search, and ask if you can set a time and date to call or meet for coffee. What you want, at least at this point, is not necessarily names and introductions but rather the contact's slant on the companies you're targeting.

Changing Careers

If you're thinking of changing careers, you need to face one cold, hard fact: it's difficult. Remember the baseball player analogy in the Target List section? To refresh your memory, years ago managers recruited for a "baseball player." Today their requirements are much more specific: plays third base, throws right-handed, hits left-handed, or steals fifty bases a year. This specificity is the result of tougher competition.

Changing careers is an easy topic for networking meetings. I once thought about getting into the solar field. Clean technology appeared to be a growing industry, so why not? Then I talked to a recruiter in my network who specialized in clean tech. I learned that while solar companies were growing, they weren't necessarily making money. One reason was that China had entered the market and begun cutting prices to win global business. Later, through my network, I talked to two people in the industry then interviewed with an executive at one of the leading clean-tech companies. From those discussions I learned:

1. The industry had matured to the point where entering it without sufficient expertise would be hard.

2. My high-tech background had little relevance to the solar field.

3. Without a strong sponsor at a clean-tech company, I had no chance of getting in. This was news to me.

In the research section of creating a target list, we discussed factors to consider in changing industries. Indisputably, you must enter through your network. Someone has got to take a chance on you — to speak up for you. If, by some incredible chance, you land a job in a field in which you have no domain expertise, the first time you make a mistake, guess what the company will blame it on: your lack of domain expertise. You simply must have it or a *very* strong sponsor, who can benefit from your talents while you learn the ropes.

I had neither solar expertise nor a sponsor in the industry, so I left the solar field to others. Instead, I focused on areas where I had domain expertise, allowing me to come from a position of strength.

Ask yourself the following questions about changing careers:

1. Why do I want to leave an industry in which I have expertise and contacts?

2. What excites me about this other industry?

3. What skills and technical knowledge give me a competitive advantage?

For the record, I once did step into a new industry. The field was growing, and not enough candidates with the appropriate background were in the pipeline. The company I joined decided that the next best thing was someone with a classic high-tech systems background. I qualified in that regard, so we had a match.

When you explore a new industry, thorough research will help you get in and succeed. Use your network to determine the most relevant online and print publications. And follow the industry's movers and shakers on Twitter. What are the hot industry trends? How do they relate to similar elements in your career? Remember to always leverage what you've done in the past.

A word of caution: if you get an interview in a new industry, acknowledge upfront that you're new to the field. Don't try to buffalo your way through based on a little reading and a few networking meetings. Instead, ask intelligent questions that reflect your understanding of the business, and relate things you've done to the company's needs. *But do not buffalo.*

Networking with Recruiters

You may become senior enough in your career to work with a recruiter, a contact that merits its own discussion. Companies often use recruiters to accelerate the hiring process. For example, they may need one to quickly form a sales team or to hire a senior executive.

There are two types of recruiters. One works in-house, as either an employee or a contractor. This person finds rank-and-file employees and first-level managers for the company. As the organization grows, it may employ one or two executive recruiters to seek out players at the vice-president level. The second type of recruiter, known as a search firm, specializes in recruiting, offering its services on an as-needed basis. Small to midsize companies that can't afford their own dedicated recruiters may hire a search firm. High-end search firms place executives at the vice-president level and above and charge a hefty fee for doing so. Depending on your current level, both types are worth your attention.

Job searchers often error in believing recruiters will treat them as customers. But these people work for the company that's paying them. You're a piece of talent who may or may not align with their client's needs. In other words, you're a commodity. You need to recognize this and the fact that recruiters owe you nothing. They'll talk to you when they have an opening for someone with your background, but they usually won't grant you an informational interview. I often tease my recruiters by telling them to call me "when they can make a buck off my body." They generally laugh, but at the same time, they know I understand their business.

To enlist the aid of a recruiter, get introduced or sponsored through your network, just as you did when meeting people in your target companies. This approach applies even more to recruiters, because many other job seekers are probably deluging them with requests for their time. When you're networking to learn the key players in your targeted companies, ask your contacts if they know of one or two top recruiters in the field, either in-house or at a search firm. Keep in mind the following hierarchy:

1. A hiring manager within a company

2. A nonhiring manager within a company who can give you the lay of the land

3. A recruiter from a search firm who can open one or two opportunities for you

4. An in-house recruiter (Keep in mind, though, that talking to this person after a job has been posted

is like replying to an online ad: the chance of success is small.)

Once you begin a dialogue with a recruiter, listen carefully to the opportunity, and decide if it's for you. If it is, he or she will likely arrange for an interview with the hiring company. If not, request more information, and offer to check your network for other job searchers who may be interested in the position. Make sure you follow up, whether you have a candidate or not. The important thing is to keep on the recruiter's radar, thus distinguishing yourself from the rest of the pack. Then, when the recruiter has an opportunity that may be a fit for you, you're more likely to receive a call.

The point is, develop a relationship with a recruiter. Whether unemployed or not, when you talk to one, consider how you can help the person. Do you know of a company that recently hired a senior executive who needs help building a team? Do you know of a company that's laid off a senior executive who needs to be replaced? Do you know of any candidates the recruiter should have on his or her radar screen? Think about how you can add value to recruiters, and they'll keep you in mind for the next opportunity.

STEP 6: BUILD A COMPELLING RESUME

This section is brief for two reasons. First, many consultants, books, and websites can instruct you on how to create a resume. Second, this document doesn't matter nearly as much as other aspects of the job-hunting process. That's because a hiring manager or HR person will spend about five to ten seconds reviewing your resume for key titles and accomplishments, rendering its carefully crafted language irrelevant. If your resume indicates you've got domain expertise and a suitable background for the job, the manager will give you a look. If not, you're unlikely to get a callback.

Still, you can boost your chances by keeping the following points in mind when creating your resume.

Make it chronological. Many resumes highlight a candidate's abilities but obscure the answers to these simple questions: What have you done for the past five to ten years? What company did you work for? What was your title? I've never understood why some very bright people make it hard to get the answers. Don't make this mistake. List the companies you've worked for and the titles you've held.

I once interviewed a candidate whose resume was hard to follow. I granted him the interview anyway because a trusted former associate had recommended him. The interview proved as confusing as the resume. I gave the candidate every opportunity to persuade me that my initial impression of him — as lacking clarity in his communications — was wrong. He failed to do, so of course I didn't invite him back.

For each position listed in your resume, focus on your accomplishments rather than on your responsibilities. Nothing gets noticed like numbers. How many people did you manage, either directly or as a member of a team? What were the metrics? How did you grow leads or sales? How did you improve efficiencies by percentage and numbers? How much revenue did the product you were responsible for produce? While you don't want your resume to resemble a scorecard, keep challenging yourself to come up with numbers.

List your awards. They're important because they tell the hiring company that you've stood out and that your superiors have recognized this. Cite only professional awards, though. Noting that you were named the most spirited member of your bowling team, perhaps to illustrate your energy and enthusiasm, won't get you very far.

Minimize your extracurricular activities by placing them at the bottom of your resume. They'll be useful only if the interviewer shares your interest in one or more of them, in which case they can be a conversation starter (this is one more reason to research your audience). But treat such activities as merely points of interest.

There's no such thing as a one-size-fits-all resume, so consider creating one to fit the job you're interviewing for. This will allow you to highlight your past positions and accomplishments relevant to that job. Do not repeat the mistake of a candidate I once interviewed. Unsure what position I was trying to fill, she brought three different resumes, leaving it to me to figure out what part of her background was relevant. I could imagine trying to manage someone like that. Needless to say, I did not invite her back.

Finally, use a template, or spend a few bucks and have a professional format your resume. In time you may want to update it on your own, but to begin with, you want a well-done resume that makes a favorable impression on potential employers.

STEP 7: ACE THE INTERVIEW

At this point in the process, your opportunities in the funnel can really accelerate. All the work you've done so far is about getting to this moment: an interview with someone who can determine, or at least influence, your future with a prospective company. Here's how to make the most of the opportunity.

Be a Preparation Sensation

Because the interview is so critical to getting a job, it has reduced many candidates, including normally poised, articulate people, to ashes. Interviewees get nervous, so they talk too much, they try too hard, or they choke on their own words, even when asked about areas they know very well. The key to avoiding such unimpressive behavior is preparation. When I was in sales, a mentor told me to invest an hour of preparation for every minute of meeting. While that may sound extreme, it's not far off the mark.

The first step in thorough preparation harks back to your student days: know the queries ahead of time, and have the answers ready. Many books, articles, and websites can provide you with common interview questions. The following are standard:

1. *What can you tell me about yourself?* This is one of my favorites. Though innocent sounding, it's the

quickest way for interviewers to end the meeting. Inexperienced candidates recite their life history, often wandering aimlessly while doing so. I've seen some labor at it for up to fifteen minutes. A number of executives have told me they've watched poor job seekers "hang themselves" (their term) on the question. Get the message? Remember, one of the most important skills in any job is effective communications. A weak answer to this question will mark you as a poor candidate.

How to score:

a. Prepare a two-minute summary of your *professional* background.

b. Highlight major decisions and key accomplishments (though it's okay to admit mistakes — see below).

c. Rehearse this summary several times using a clock or stopwatch. You must deliver your answer crisply or your interview is done.

2. *What accomplishment are you most proud of?* Again, this is a quick disqualifier if you don't nail the answer. Many candidates wander around, casually talking about several projects they've participated in.

How to score:

a. Prepare three stories about yourself in advance. Each should include:

  i. The situation.

  ii. Your actions (be specific if you were part of a team).

iii. The result, such as lower costs or increased revenues. To be most effective, include numbers or percentages in your answer.

b. Practice telling these stories — in the shower, in the car, while exercising — until you're comfortable with them and your delivery is flawless.

3. *Which of your accomplishments relates to the requirements of this job (a derivative of the question above)?* To answer this effectively, know what attributes the company is looking for, which you can determine by reviewing the job specifications in advance. Obtain them in the following ways:

a. While we've emphasized many times not to pursue a job through a company's web site, sometimes your network will lead you to an opportunity that does, in fact, find itself posted. If you're applying for a job posted on the company's website or on a job site such as theladders.com, LinkedIn, or monster.com, it will usually provide the job specifications. Read them thoroughly, and use them to help create your stories. In other words, map the stories to the requirements.

b. If you're at a high enough level to be working with a recruiter, ask for job specifications. He or she will be glad to provide them. Generally, the specs will take up four to six pages. Find out which ones are really important to the hiring manager. Bear in mind that key requirements may change during the recruiting process. What was important one month may be irrelevant the next because the manager's key problems have changed. I've got a "magic" question that'll uncover what's top-of-mind to a particular hiring manager. These people are like the rest of us: what they don't have yet consumes them. So I ask the recruiter (or the company's HR person), "Of the candidates you've seen so far, what's been missing?" The answer will reveal the job's key requirement and give you one-up on the competition. I once asked this question of a recruiter interviewing me for a vice president of marketing position. He answered, "The candidates we've seen so far don't have a deep understanding of solutions marketing. They're all telling us how to pitch products." Guess what? I walked into the office of the hiring executive vice president with a story about how I'd created success in the past with solutions.

How to score:
a. Similar to question 1, have your stories ready.
b. Practice them, and be able to deliver flawlessly.

4. *What's your greatest weakness?* This is almost like an intelligence test. If you vividly describe a weakness that disqualifies you from the job, you're done. Many candidates recognize this, so they come up with stock answers, such as, "I work too hard," or "I'm too much of a perfection-ist." These replies are almost as bad as those that automatically disqualify a candidate. Thus, the question provides you with another chance to distinguish yourself from the competition. The

hiring manager understands you'll make mistakes. You merely want to make clear that you *will* correct them.

Mistakes are a part of life. As a mentor once said, "They're why God made erasers." Think about a torpedo launched from a submarine. Because of the water's motion, the earth's gravitational pull, and other factors, the torpedo won't head directly for its target. Like a bat, it'll emit sonar waves to acquire the feedback necessary to adjust its course. This will happen multiple times as the torpedo traverses its path. Finally, it will hit its target.

How to score:
a. Turn the question to your advantage by choosing a trait related to the job but not critical to your success at it.

b. Then describe the feedback you've received, and explain how you're using it to improve.

I can use myself as an example here. I once received feedback from my team that I wasn't paying enough attention to detail. Since then I've done two things to correct this shortcoming: I've hired people who do pay careful attention to detail, and I've scheduled enough time so I can too. I've heard I'm improving, but I realize I still have work to do.

In an interview, I could use this weakness, and my attempts to correct it, to my advantage by noting that I can be coached, not just by my superiors — which everyone expects — but by my subordinates as well.

Also, I act on feedback. In this case, I took steps to improve my performance. Finally, I could say I'm self-aware enough to know I have flaws. But none, I might add, is fatal enough to prevent me from doing this job.

As I've said, the best way to score in an interview is to prepare for questions ahead of time. Another thing to prepare for is making conversation, including small talk that goes beyond the weather. It's important that you be a good conversationalist, including with the receptionist who says something while you're waiting in the lobby and with the secretary who's escorting you to the meeting. By being a conversationalist, you connect with the individual and create an opportunity to stand out from your competition.

When you meet the interviewer, having something worthwhile to say will set you apart, while putting both of you more at ease.

Here are some areas for conversation:

1. *Current events.* I used to read only the sports and business sections of the newspaper. Later, however, I realized a lot of other things were going on in the world. By reading about them, I became better at conversing, both socially and professionally. You can personalize the news to become even more engaging. For example, you could ask your host if he or she read about hurricane Sandy, and then note that it forced your daughter to cancel her plans to run in the New York marathon.

2. *Company updates.* Read all you can about the organization you're applying to. I've interviewed

people who didn't know what the company did. On the other hand, some have asked insightful questions about relevant trends and about how the company was positioning itself to capture greater market share. These interviewees impressed me. As suggested earlier, use your network to help acquaint you with the organization.

3. If you're applying for an executive position, you may wind up talking to a high-profile individual. Research the executive through Google or by querying your network contacts. In addition to weightier information, find out what the person's hobbies and favorite charities are. These can lead to an interesting conversation.

   a. Your network and informational interviews can help you here, too. As you meet with people in your network, you're getting insights not only into your target companies, but also into their executives as well (remember the Hiring Manager column on your target list?). Many informational interviews gained through my network helped me avert disaster by providing insights into a prospective boss.

   b. Refer back to the section on conducting research via the Internet and LinkedIn. These tools can help you access the backgrounds of prospective hiring managers as well as gain insights into their companies. Through LinkedIn, you can request people's insights into your opportunity. I've often met people at this website who were only too happy to help.

4. *Casual stories.* In addition to preparing stories for your potential interview questions (see above), have a few ready for casual conversation. Think about something you've done or experienced recently that can serve as an icebreaker. Did you plan any trips? Did your clever kids teach you anything?

You've done your homework through networking. You've learned about the company and hiring manager. You've done your reading and research so you're ready for some small talk. You can do still more to fine-tune your preparation.

Organize all your preparation notes and any items in your memory bank. I like to prepare two pages. The first consists of points I want to make in the interview, including stories describing my greatest accomplishments and any skills relevant to the job I'm applying for. If the points I want to make don't come up in the interview, I can make them, politely, toward the end.

If you get past the first portion of the interview, distinguish yourself from the competition by asking well prepared questions. Many books and websites list such inquiries, but here are a few you can use with anyone from a hiring manager to an HR representative to a potential peer:

1. What do you like best about working here?

2. If I get a review in a year that says my performance is outstanding, what have I accomplished?

3. Where will the company's future growth come from?

4. How will your company handle the rising costs of Chinese labor, given that it does 20 percent of its engineering in China? This is one of many possible questions to ask after referring to your notes and seeing what needs clarifying. You can also show you've done your homework by asking questions that begin with, "I see that your company has...."

Ask no more than four or five questions, and don't make them rapid-fire. Have a conversation, and enjoy yourself. Sometimes you'll learn things you can use in subsequent interviews.

Get to the Location on Time

You'd be surprised how many applicants are tardy for an interview. Don't you be. Arriving late not only will get you off on the wrong foot, but also could lead to your feeling harried and nervous the entire session.

A couple measures can help get you there on time:

1. Obtain directions ahead of time. A number of Internet mapping services—including two of the most popular, Google Maps and Mapquest—can help accomplish this.

2. Drive to your meeting's location beforehand to avoid surprises on interview day. If possible, do a test run at the same time of day you'll be driving to your interview, so you can account for traffic.

On the actual drive, take your cell phone so if something delays you, you can at least notify the receptionist or the hiring manager's assistant. Pull over to make the call. This will allow you to relax and hold a stronger conversation, in addition to minimizing the chances of an accident due to distracted driving. Also, know who to ask for when you arrive.

I once had an interview with an executive and didn't know that his assistant would be out that day, and the HR representative was scheduled to greet me instead. Because it took a while for the receptionist and me to resolve the misunderstanding, I was late and did not make a good impression. Think I got invited back? You're right, I didn't. The lesson is confirm with the individual making your appointment whom to ask for at the reception desk: the hiring manager, an HR person, a coordinator, or the assistant. Don't leave this one to chance.

What to Wear

Your attire will depend on the level of the vacant position, the culture, and the location of the company. Stories abound of a candidate being overdressed, underdressed, or just plain inappropriately dressed for an interview.

For men meeting with an executive recruiter, a sports coat, collared shirt, and slacks are generally acceptable. Women should dress as business professionals. Slacks are fine but no jeans. Former HP CEO Carly Fiorina always impressed me with how she dressed. Sharp, feminine, but nothing low cut. Show your respect for the recruiter by arriving well dressed. I work in Silicon Valley, the land of business casual, but for job interviews, most candidates dress up.

You can ask your company contact how to dress. In some business cultures, men should wear suits to their interviews. In others, suits or even jackets will make the interviewer uncomfortable. Moreover, the requirements for an engineering job at a Silicon Valley start-up will be different from a marketing position with IBM in New York. So ask.

Follow Up

I'm amazed at how many job candidates don't follow up. Whether it's writing a thank-you note, making a phone call, or performing a few tasks after a networking meeting, do your follow-up. It may be hard to put yourself out there, but do it. Here are some areas that need follow-up:

1. After meeting with people in your network, you'll almost always have to do some follow-up. For example, some of them may have offered to do a few things for you. It's not up to them to follow up on their own. No matter how wonderful you are, they're not there to serve you. *You* must follow through with *them*. Send e-mails indicating which offers appealed to you most (perhaps it was an introduction to the head of finance at ABC Company). No matter how many things people offered to do, pick no more than two that are likely to have an impact.

2. Via e-mail, a friend introduces you to someone in power who can help in your job search. Now the ball's in your court; you must call the person. That'll probably be hard because you've got no idea how this stranger will react. Yet you must make the call because your friend certainly won't do it for you.

3. Learn to write thank-you notes to all the people who help you. Get a box of high-quality stationery — nothing cheap, please — and *handwrite* a thank-you. Do this for interviews and networking meetings, as well as for any favors rendered along the way. Naturally, e-mail is better for back-and-forth follow-up, as in items 1 and 2 above. But for a flat-out thank-you, nothing beats a handwritten note.

4. Continue connecting with people you've already contacted. I discussed earlier how I keep a spreadsheet of everyone I've talked to during my journey. I include name, title, company, and the last time I communicated with the person. As I also mentioned earlier, I connect with people on this list regularly. It's amazing how you *can* go to the well more than once. People appreciate the continued correspondence, and the renewed connection may spur additional thoughts from them, including new leads and contacts.

Don't think that once you've connected, your network contacts will remember you. They aren't computers; they're people. Ever wonder why Apple, American Express, and Eveready spend so much money on advertising? It's about reinforcing the message, and you must do the same.

5. Many candidates assume that the next step after an interview is to wait for a response. Wrong. Let's say the meeting went well, but the hiring manager said something like, "We're looking at several candidates. I'll get back to you in a week regarding the next step." Send a thank-you immediately, let a week go by, and then check in via e-mail. The hand written message you send can be friendly but assertive. I've used something like this:

Chuck—

I really enjoyed our meeting last week regarding the VP of marketing position in your organization. We discussed your need for someone who understands how to develop solutions and create buzz for your products, and then we reviewed my expertise in these areas. You indicated that we should reconnect in a week to discuss the next step. I'll call you then to see how you'd like to proceed.

Regards,

Bob

That's simple and professional, doesn't sell too hard, and states your intentions.

In the follow-up call you promised, you can say something like, "I really enjoyed our time together. Assuming you decided to continue our dialogue about how I can help your organization, what would be the next step?"

You've done two things here:

1. Reinforced that you're interested in the job. Don't play hard-to-get early in the game. It's like dating; people want people who want them.

2. Acknowledged that no matter how well the interview went, the hiring manager still makes the next call. This is a powerful tactic. If the manager feels you're a miss, you've given him or her an easy out. If you're a borderline candidate, you've let the manager continue to evaluate you. If you're a hit, you've shown you realize he or she is talking to other candidates and you're not a slam dunk. A sharp hiring manager will conclude you're still interviewing at other companies — meaning his or her competition.

The rest of the phone call might go like this:

> *Interviewer: I like what you bring to the table, so I'll arrange for you to talk to three other members of my team.*

> *Candidate: That would be great. For my own planning purposes, when do you think that might happen?*

> *Interviewer: Within the next couple weeks. I'll have my assistant arrange it.*

> *Candidate: Your assistant — is that Judy who set up our meeting today?*

> *Interviewer: Yes, it is.*

> **Candidate:** *If I don't hear anything, would it be okay to connect with her by the end of the week, to make sure nothing has fallen through the crack?*

This last question is a powerful tool. Interviewers usually don't share with candidates how they really feel about them because they don't want to put themselves in an uncomfortable position. They feel being too positive will sap their power. If they don't think you're a fit, they risk listening to you try to sell yourself. If they consider you borderline, they want time to think things over. The question, asking for permission to proceed, cuts through all these situations. If you're on the border and the interviewer has been playing with you, you just got a ticket to proceed to the next step. If you're a miss, it will flush out very quickly through Judy. If you're a hit, the interviewer will make sure everyone is saved the embarrassment by talking to Judy as soon as you're done with that day's interview.

Follow up with Judy at the end of the week, and then don't let her off the hook. Particularly at higher levels, the Judy's of the world are adept at insulating themselves. You must be relentless to break through to them. I've called as many as fifteen times to catch a "Judy." Because a lot of office phones have caller ID, my line at home has a blocker so people at the other end can't tell who I am. Curiosity killed the cat, and it might get Judy to pick up the phone. The best times to call either her or the hiring manager are:

- 7:30 a.m. to 8:30 a.m., before that nine o'clock meeting kicks in.

- Thirty minutes before or after the 12:00 p.m. to 1:00 p.m. lunch hour, when many people allow themselves time for e-mail and paperwork.

- 4:30 p.m. to 5:30 p.m., at workday's end, after all the meetings have taken place.

Following up after the interview is one of the most important components in the job-search process. You *must* do it to get to the next step and eventually an offer. Managers have so many problems they must solve immediately that hiring someone who won't come aboard for months, and then will require additional months of training before producing results, is just not their highest priority. Many candidates believe that if the hiring manager really wants them, he or she will naturally follow up. Not true. Part of the drill is displaying your drive and determination to get the job. Show it by taking the initiative.

Case Study—Interviewing Skills

My daughter Kate was seeking an internship during her senior year in college. She'd pursued several opportunities that hadn't borne fruit. Knowing this, I called her one day to ask what she could do better to land one of these internships. She walked me through her process and, at the end, concluded she hadn't felt well prepared for the questions. She'd stumbled around, failed to make her points, and given weak answers. After overhearing our conversation, my wife suggested that if I couldn't help my own daughter, I had no business writing this book.

I advised Kate that perhaps she needed more structured preparation for the questions. I suggested she list the three greatest strengths she'd bring to the internship. She would essentially prepare for the question, which of your accomplishments relates to the requirements of this job? After she did so, I asked her to create a story for each, showcasing the strength. I said the stories should state the situation, her approach, and the result. Kate had an advantage in that many of her initial interviews were being conducted over the phone. She could write out her stories in detail, and no one would know she was essentially reading from her notes. Kate, being very creative, came up with wonderful stories highlighting her abilities and relevant accomplishments. Next came the tricky part. I said that, for every question asked in the interview that was similar to "which of your accomplishments…," unless the answer was a no-brainer, she should relate it to one of her strengths and its associated story.

My daughter called three days later, after her next interview, and said the new method had given her much more confidence. She'd had no problem digging up opportunities but needed a little leverage to get to the finish line. The new approach so energized her that she created a couple other stories, including one that, with humor, highlighted a weakness and showed how she was overcoming it. Two weeks later, my daughter had received three offers for internships. She arranged her schedule to handle two of them, while she referred the other to a friend who hadn't been so lucky.

STEP 8: GETTING OFFERS AND CLOSING THE DEAL

Many people view the closing process as combative effort, in which each party competes for what it wants and collapses at the end, exhausted if not dead or wounded. But it needn't be this way. Ideally, if the company and candidate both want a deal, the hiring manager will try to satisfy the candidate's needs while working within his or her own constraints. This should be a cooperative exercise, but unfortunately, sometimes it's not. In such cases, the company will essentially tell an applicant, "This is our offer. We have back-up candidates ready to go, so take it, or leave it." Many job seekers encounter this attitude, which, in my experience, reflects the company's culture and signals the place may not be the best to work at after all.

Compensation

A top concern of most candidates is salary. What's the company willing to pay, and what's reasonable to ask for? Determining the appropriate salary for a given position will require a little research. There's an old saying, "In God we trust, all others bring data." So data is extremely valuable in deciding what salary to ask for. Some excellent resources can help you. The first is the Internet. My favorite site for salary information is Glassdoor.com. It displays salaries for a particular company, by position, at each of its locations. The site shows not only the average salary for each position, but also a range of salaries so you can see the spectrum available to you. While you might naturally want the highest salary listed, you must realize that the more money a position pays, the more qualifications it's likely to require. You're looking for the right salary to start with.

Another resource for gathering salary information is your network, particularly people in your industry and area of expertise who may be a level or two above you. These individuals probably have hired people like you. Feel free to share what you've discovered about salaries in your research, and ask them what their experience suggests on the subject. This will be good information to have before going into salary negotiations (which we cover shortly).

Your prospective employer may ask what your current compensation is. But before stating it, you might want to know the company's salary range for the position you're seeking. An old adage says the side that provides the information first, loses. But I believe direct questions generally deserve direct answers, and this is one of those times. If asked what your current compensation is, state it, no matter what you know or don't know about the company's salary range. After providing this information, you may ask if it's in line with what the company has in mind. If you've done your research, you'll have an idea before you inquire, but ask anyway just to be sure. If the answer is yes, simply continue with the process. If no, inquire if there's any wiggle room. An employer who wants a candidate will usually find a way to make the compensation work. If this company isn't willing to do so, you need to decide whether it's the place for you. While you may feel pressured to get a job to pay the bills, you don't want to be looking for one again shortly after accepting an offer.

On the other hand, keep in mind that an employer's flexibility often depends on the company's location, the industry it's in, and the state of the economy. For example, in Silicon Valley and New York, when the economy's hot, the competition for software engineers is keen and an organization's flexibility greater. In other locations, other industries, and in tougher economic times, not so much.

In addition to salary, other types of compensation, like bonuses and stock options, may be part of the package. If you've never received these, a higher-level network contact can advise you on issues such as whether you're at a level to receive them and how much you can typically expect.

Relocation and Commuting

In addition to compensation, you may need to negotiate other items. What if you're located a distance from the office? If you're far enough away to need relocation, be up front about it. Or perhaps the company will *require* you to relocate. Then you must decide if you're willing to move. If you are, ask whether moving assistance or help in deferring costs is available. The higher your level, the greater the relocation package.

Your approach will be different if your distance from the office would mean an inconvenient commute but not relocation. Moving and its related expenses won't be an issue, but your well-being on the job will (or should) be. We earlier covered the commute as part of your job criteria and suggested that you think about a travel boundary. Let's say the company's location from your home fell within it but was not ideal. You pursued the opportunity, but now that you're about to sign an offer letter, you may want to discuss the commute. Ask the hiring manager about the possibility of working from home occasionally. Your chances will be greater if the job requires little interaction with coworkers (think telesales or customer support) than if it's office-centric. Once again, a higher-level manager in your network can guide you.

A final word on the commute: if the company agrees to let you work from home on occasion, and you do accept its offer, stay in the office 100 percent of the time for the first three months so you can fully integrate into your new environment.

Vacation and Education

Another element of compensation is vacation. Eligibility generally depends on time in service, while the amount allotted is determined by seniority — so the subject is pretty much nonnegotiable. But not entirely. If you've got a planned vacation coming up as you finalize the job offer, you may be able to take it in exchange for accelerating your start date. Or you may merely make it part of the offer package.

How about education? Perhaps you're working toward a college degree, advanced or otherwise, and your current company is paying your tuition. Ask if the new organization will do the same. You may find out it does, but only for top performers. Rather than waiting in line for such recognition, make reimbursement part of the offer package.

Negotiate the Offer

You'd be wise to limit your negotiation requests and to keep them simple enough for the hiring manager to resolve with a phone call. A laundry list of items requiring a good deal of haggling within the company might tick some people off before you even start the job.

The negotiation process itself is usually simple. You state your requirements, and the hiring company makes an oral offer, sometimes followed by a discussion. You digest the terms for a couple days then return and agree to them or make a counteroffer (based on research and consultation with your network contacts). The hiring company comes back with a final offer that you either accept or decline. A detail or two may need refinement, but you don't want a back-and-forth struggle that leads to an ultimate deal but leaves a bad taste in everyone's mouth. Not a good beginning.

Occasionally you'll be lucky enough to receive competing offers from more than one company. Obviously, you'll evaluate them to determine which is best for you. But things aren't always that simple.

While you'd probably welcome any job offer, you prefer one company to the others. What if "second-place" makes an offer before the preferred organization does? In handling this situation, it's perfectly okay to give different messages to the two companies:

1. Inform your top pick that another company has tendered an offer or is about to make one. If it's truly interested in you, your preferred choice will accelerate the offer process. If it's not, then at least you'll know.

2. Tell your second pick you have another offer coming and want to evaluate all the data — that is, the written offers — before making a decision. The company likely will respect your desire to make an informed choice, but it'll probably have backup candidates and want an answer as soon as possible. You can reasonably stall for up to a week, but no longer.

When you've made your choice, inform both companies but keep in mind that no offer is an offer until you have it in writing. So don't turn down a job (or resign from one you already have) until you've gotten a written offer letter. A well-known company once gave me an oral offer and indicated a letter would be forthcoming. I waited a week, then two weeks, all the while staying in touch with the hiring manager. When the letter failed to arrive, he indicated it had been lost in the system. I was able to shrug this off because I held a good job at Hewlett-Packard, which, fortunately, I hadn't resigned when I received the "offer." As I said, wait till you get an offer in writing before doing anything drastic. (Incidentally, two months later, three recruiters called me regarding the same opportunity.)

If possible, take some time off before starting your new role. After all, getting the job is cause for celebration. In addition, you may want to reflect on things, such as your new daily routine and what you'd like to accomplish in the first ninety days on the job. Also, your new company likely will need time to get business cards printed for you and set up your workspace and equipment. Typically, one or two weeks are a reasonable window, especially if you're unemployed. If the new company insists it needs you immediately, cultivate a little goodwill by jumping right in.

Conclusion

Over the years, I've grown my career while cycling through companies. My employer today isn't the one I had when I started this book. Talk about stuff happening. I'd flown to corporate headquarters on the East Coast, planning to spend the week in a series of meetings. But on the morning of the first day, my boss summoned me to his office and informed me my position had been eliminated. The company flew me back to the West Coast—first class, at least—that afternoon. Fortunately, I knew what to do, got myself going, and quickly landed a position even better than my previous one.

As of this writing, many people—from entry-level hopefuls to new college graduates to business professionals—are struggling to find work in a difficult economy, one in which the competition for fewer jobs is steep. In desperation, the unemployed are examining job boards and sending resumes by the bushel, hoping to hear back from someone. But you can position yourself for getting work in any economy. Managers still need the best talent, and you must let them know who you are before they resort to recruiters and job postings. The guidelines in this book can give you an advantage over the competition and help you get a job that's even superior to the one you left. You undoubtedly have bills to pay and mouths to feed. Nevertheless, I encourage you to think of the job hunt as a game. To come out ahead in any contest, be it tennis or Monopoly, you must play to win. And I encourage you to do just that as you search for a new and better job.

Case Study—Tying it all Together

I met an extraordinary individual who I think provides the best, final case study highlighting how to tie these lessons together. I was on a tour at Catholic Charities of Santa Clara County in the heart of the Silicon Valley. Greg Kepferle, the organization's CEO, was showing me the facility and the work being done by the various agencies. While Catholic Charities receives some money from the church, the organization services over 40,000 people of all religions by providing food, elder care, youth programs, and other services for those less fortunate throughout the region.

During our tour, Greg introduced me to Eila Latif, who runs the organization's job search function called For Work. I was struck by Eila's enthusiasm for her job and the joy she took in helping her clients. When I asked how long she had been in her role, she playful joked with me that she had been with the same organization, in the same role, in the same office for twenty years! What really impressed me was that Eila's job-search clients all had one thing in common. They all suffered from mental illness. Imagine how difficult a job search is when you are combating a headwind like that.

I spoke in detail with Eila and learned more about the mental illness her clients had to endure. Some of them had genetic challenges and would need to deal with those handicaps forever. Others were like you and me, where a traumatic event, such as the death of a loved one or even a job loss brought on the condition. Eila talked about her staff and her clients as if they were her own children. Now, sometimes we aren't always pleased with our children, but I could plainly see the passion Eila had for what she did.

Most non-profit organizations have high turnover and need time to find qualified staff and continually ramp them up. Not Eila. In addition to her twenty years of tenure, most of her team has been with her for anywhere from three to twelve years. The work they do to help their clients secure jobs is truly remarkable. Through one to one counseling sessions and scalable programs like ten hours per week of classroom instruction, Focus For Work uses principles very similar to what we have covered to have a success rate that is almost triple for the industry.

Focus For Work initially works with its clients to identify their career goals and job preferences. The clients review what skills they have and what their target jobs look like. Then the Focus For Work counselor will work with the client to identify the appropriate companies he or she should pursue. The process is similar to the assessment plan we discussed in chapter 4.

Afterwards the Focus For Work team develops a networking plan with the client. Similar to our discussion in Chapter 5, Eila's staff members review whom the client should network with to get into his or her target companies. In addition, they have done extensive networking to pave the way for opportunities for their clients. For example, one of the staff arranged to meet a facilities manager at the HP Pavilion, a major venue in San Jose for sports events and concerts. They made an initial arrangement for Focus For Work to provide candidates for selling tickets and concessions. The first year resulted in a number of Focus For Work candidates and was so successful that Focus For Work now gets a call from the SAP Arena each year announcing hiring plans and requests that Eila's team recommends the appropriate candidates to be interviewed for the positions.

During the job search process, the Focus For Work team works with candidates on resume writing, interviewing, and closing for an offer. You can imagine that sometimes this population presents unique challenges for the counselors. Once when a counselor was driving a client to an interview, the client asked if it was OK to smoke pot beforehand. Clearly not an issue most of us would encounter.

Eila related a number of success stories to me that morning. Her team helped a woman get a job at a florist as a cashier. Just over a year later, that woman took over the business and approached Eila for candidates to hire. Local tech heavyweights Cisco and Google regularly hire from Focus For Work each year in roles from cafeteria worker to full-fledged developer. If a candidate overcoming this kind of resistance can land successfully in a job, you can too.

9/18
③

CPSIA information can be obtained at www.ICGtesting.com
Printed in the USA
LVOW07s2358260815

451718LV00011B/83/P